Soaring With Excellence

Guides for Spiritual Growth

By

Deborah Cox

© 2003 by Deborah Cox. All rights reserved.

No part of this book may be reproduced, stored in a retrieval system, or transmitted by any means, electronic, mechanical, photocopying, recording, or otherwise, without written permission from the author.

ISBN: 1-4107-8511-4 (e-book)
ISBN: 1-4107-8510-6 (Paperback)
ISBN: 1-4107-8509-2 (Dust Jacket)

This book is printed on acid free paper.

1stBooks - rev. 09/17/03

Dedication

This book has been a sweet labor of love dedicated to my Lord and Savior, Jesus Christ, who brought me out of darkness and into the light. He has allowed me the privilege of participating in the building of His Kingdom by sharing His thoughts and practical instruction for daily living through years of leading small groups, which became the basis for these written guides.

I must thank all of those who have passed through my classes over the years. Whether you were in my Sunday school classes, youth groups, Singles group, workplace Bible studies, or my home groups… you were, and continue to be, the charge of my life. Not only am I *charged* with responsibility for your growth, but you provide the charge that ignites my life. There have been some particularly electrifying times for me. There were those times I prayed with some of you to receive Christ as your Savior, and times when I sat on the front pew and watched your baptism. I was there when some of you preached your first sermons. I wept with joy when you told me you were surrendering to full-time missions. I have seen many of you blossom into the leaders God destined you to become. I have seen so many of you grow up before me, both physically and spiritually. What a blessing it has been for me to be a part of your lives!

I must also thank all those teachers, pastors, mentors, family and friends who have deposited greatly into my life and soul.

And finally, this book is dedicated to all of you whom I will never meet this side of heaven whom God has purposefully placed this book into your hands. May it bless you, enrich you, stir you, and leave you hungry for more!

Deborah Cox

Acknowledgements

All Scripture references used taken from *New International Version,* Colorado Springs, International Bible Society (1978, 1984)

June Seabaugh, Editor

Scripture References

Matthew 7:21-23
1 Cor. 12:31
2 Peter 1:5-11
Daniel 6:10
Proverbs 10:9
Romans 1:18-20
Job 1:8
Job 2:9-11
2 Peter 1:2-4
Romans 12:1-2
2 Corinthians 3:18
Ecclesiastes 12:13-14
Proverbs 1:7
Ecclesiastes 2:10-11
Proverbs 2:1-8
Proverbs 3:5-6
James 1:26
Proverbs 18:21
Proverbs 21:23
Proverbs 4:24
Proverbs 18:6
Proverbs 20:19
Proverbs 12:25
Proverbs 16:24
Proverbs 15:1
Colossians 3:17
Mark 11:25
Mark 5:18-19
Proverbs 20:7
Proverbs 4:3-4
Proverbs 22:6
Proverbs 29:17
Colossians 3:18-21
Matthew 5:13
Matthew 5:13-16

John 10:14-15
Gal. 6:3-5
1 Thessalonians 2:10-12
Ephesians 6:10-13
Matthew 6:27
Phillipians 4:6-7
Matthew 7:13-14
Matthew 6:1-4
Mark 8:34
Romans 3:25a
Mark 7:1-3
Acts 15:5-11
Romans 3:20-24
Romans 6:6-7
Romans 6:20-23
Romans 6:14-19
John 19:19-22
Romans 6:12-13
Romans 15:17-18
Colossians 3:22-4:1
Matthew 5:17-20
Hebrews 13:17
2 Thessalonians 1:8-10
John 19:1-3
John 10:10
Galatians 6:1
Romans 14:17-18
Proverbs 20:1
1 Cor. 6:13b
1 Cor. 18-20
Ephesians 5:3
Ephesians 4:26-27
Galatians 1:3-5
2 Thessalonians 1:3-4
2 Thessalonians 1:5-7

1 Thessalonians 2:3-4
Matthew 7:1-3
Matthew 7:26-29
1 Timothy 6:10
Mark 8:35-38
Mark 10:17, 21-22
Romans 1:16-17
Romans 12:9-10
John 3:16
Luke 18:17
1 Samuel 16:7
Romans 1:14
Romans 12:4-5
Romans 12:14-16
Ephesians 5:1-4
Romans 15:14-16
John 4:28-30
Matthew 28:18-20

Colossians 4:5-6
Colossians 4:7-9
Matthew 5:6
Luke 24:45-48
Luke 24:4-8
1 Thessalonians 2:6b-8
Matthew 7:7-12
1 Thessalonians 3:11-13
Matthew 15:32
Mark 6:34-37
Mark 6:38-42
John 4:23-24
Matthew 6:5-7
Matthew 6:9-13
John 19:30
Jeremiah 29:11
2 Thessalonians 2:1-2
Revelation 3:20-21

Table of Contents

Dedication	iii
Acknowledgements	v
Scripture References	vii
Do We Know Each Other?	1
Am I Striving or Settling?	3
The Excellence Formula	5
Works Every Time	9
Solid Oak Christians	11
What's Your Excuse?	13
Can I Handle Abundance?	15
Can I Handle Loss?	17
I Can Do This!	19
Is My Life a Living Sacrifice?	21
I'm Not There, But I'm On My Way	25
Am I Walking in Wisdom?	27
Am I Chasing the Wind?	29
How's Your Spiritual Report Card?	31
All Means All, Not Some	33
Loose Lips and Wagging Tongues	35
To Speak or Not to Speak, That is the Question	37
Junk, Gibberish, or Juicy?	39
Helpful, Hopeful, and Healing	41
Attitudes are Revealing	43
Why Should I Forgive Them?	45
Start With Your Family	47
It All Starts at Home	49
Perfect Parenting Tips	51
Too Much Togetherness	53
Pass the Salt, Please	55
Preserve and Illuminate	57
I Want to be in His Flock	59
The "Why" Behind My "Do"	61
Come On, You Can Do It!	63
The Big "D"	65

Living Without Worry, Stress, or Anxiety…Can It Really Be Done?!... 67
Following the Leader 69
People Pleasing Avenue.. 71
High Profile, Low Profile, or No Profile?................................. 73
Pick that Up and Follow Me 77
Atoning Blood... 79
But We've Always Done It That Way!..................................... 81
But They Are Not Like Us! 85
What are the Rules?.. 87
I'm Not Your Slave... 89
Do I Really Want to Be God's Slave? 91
Are You Obeying Your Master?... 93
The Sign of Authority 95
Give God the Reins... 97
Acknowledge Your Power Source.. 99
Who's the Boss? 101
Do I Have To?... 103
Who's In Charge Here? 105
No Middle Ground.. 107
Is That a Whip in My Hand?... 109
Don't Let the Devil Sneak Up on You! 111
Caught in a Trap.. 113
Don't Major on Minor Issues... 115
Under the Influence or Under His Influence?......................... 117
Sharing My Body with God.. 119
Setting Sexual Standards.. 121
That Makes me So Mad! Now What?..................................... 123
Heavenly 911 125
Spiritual Work-Out 127
God Has It All Under Control... 129
The Real Deal 131
Specks and Planks... 133
Crash Landing... 135
Storm Warning!... 137
Clean Heart Check 139
Buy Now, Pray Later 141
Win or Lose…No Draw.. 143
How Much Is This Going to Cost? 145

From First to Last	147
Love Walking	149
Is It Really Love?	151
The Faith of A Child	153
Is Your Heart Showing?	155
I Have an Obligation	157
Let's Work Together	159
Can I Pass This Love Test?	163
Who Do People See When They Look At Me?	165
I Have Been Called	167
Do You Want To Hear Something Really Good?	169
Take My Name…and Use It!	171
Bringing "Outsiders" Inside	173
Getting Involved	175
Anybody Hungry?	179
It All Makes Sense Now	181
In the Right Place at the Right Time	183
Easy Does It	185
A Good Relationship with Him Makes for Better Relationships with Them	187
Overflowing Love	189
Nobody Could Love Them…Could They?	191
Love Seeds	193
See a Need, Meet a Need	195
Leftovers Anyone?	197
Check Your Worship Meter	199
Listen to Me, Look at Me	201
Praying His Way	203
The End Was Just the Beginning	207
Crystal Ball or Lord of All?	209
If I Only Knew About Tomorrow	211
Please Open The Door!	213
About the Author	217

Do We Know Each Other?

"Not everyone who says to me, 'Lord, Lord', will enter the kingdom of heaven, but only he who does the will of my Father who is in heaven. Many will say to me on that day, 'Lord, Lord, did we not prophesy in your name, and in your name drive out demons and perform many miracles?' Then I will tell them plainly, 'I never knew you. Away from me, you evildoers!'" (Matthew 7:21-23)

There are probably just about as many people in hell who "thought" they were Christians as there are people that knew they weren' t. That' s a scary thought. Religion does not secure salvation for us. Going to church does not make us righteous. We can' t hide behind our denominational banner. We can' t get to heaven on our parent' s salvation experience. We can' t follow a written set of rules and expect that to be enough. The rich, young ruler found that out. ***(Matthew 19:16-22)***

Jesus' words in verse 23 are sobering. *"Then I will tell them plainly, 'I never knew you.'"* You might be thinking, "That doesn' t seem right. Jesus knows everything and everyone." But He is not speaking here of having a <u>knowledge</u> of those who were addressing Him. He was saying that He did not have a <u>relationship with them.</u> A lot of people like to equate their knowledge of Christ with a saving relationship with Him. Most of us know who holds the office of the President of the United States, but few of us have a personal relationship with him. Many people like to rely on their belief in God as their ticket to heaven. That doesn' t work either. Even Satan and his demons believe in God.

And there are others who want to place their good deeds on the scales to show themselves worthy of salvation. That won' t do it, either, because <u>one</u> sin outweighs all the good things you have ever done or ever will do. What is it then? What can give me the assurance of salvation that I long for? Our faith in Jesus Christ, our acceptance of His sacrificial gift to us, our repentant heart, our personal relationship with Him secures our place in the kingdom. His blood, not our good works, makes us righteous.

Do you know Him personally? Does He know you? Are you relying on religious trappings to cover your sin? Or, does the blood of your personal Savior cover you?

Prayer thought: Holy Spirit, reveal to me the condition of my heart. I do not want to stand before You and hear You say, "I never knew you."

Am I Striving or Settling?

"And now I will show you the most excellent way." (1 Cor. 12:31)

One year during a revival in our church several groups were asked to prepare the evening meal each night for the evangelist and his family, as well as the rest of our church family. Since I was the youth leader, I was responsible for "Youth Night." We decided on a Mexican meal, and I assigned each person a different item to bring for the preparation. They did a very good job. However, there was one young man who was assigned to bring shredded lettuce and cheese for the tacos. He didn' t show. I called his home just prior to serving time, and his dad said that he had gone somewhere with his mother. I hung up the phone and said, "Well, I guess we' ll just have to be lettuceless." As it turned out there was some lettuce in the church refrigerator. And, yes, we could have made it through the meal without lettuce and the meal would have been "good enough," but it would not have been "excellent."

A lot of us live our Christian lives the same way. We are missing a few ingredients, but we' ve convinced ourselves that our lives are "good enough," and we don' t strive anymore for excellence, but settle for mediocrity. For example, maybe our language or our conversations sometimes are lacking the ingredient of restraint or self-control. Or maybe our behavior with our family members is lacking patience. Maybe our attitude with certain people is lacking kindness. Perhaps our choices of entertainment are lacking godliness. It doesn' t mean that we are not Christians, it just means that our Christian lives are missing a few key ingredients at times. They may be good enough for other people to recognize them as Christian lives, but not excellent to the point that others are asking us for the recipe. We are to be continually striving toward the excellence that is within us in the person of the Holy Spirit. After all, God gave us His best. We should give Him ours.

Prayer thought: Lord, show me the missing ingredients in my life. Help me not to be satisfied with being a mediocre Christian, but to strive continually for the excellence that You desire from me.

The Excellence Formula

"For this very reason, make every effort to add to your faith goodness; and to goodness, knowledge; and to knowledge, self-control; and to self-control, perseverance; and to perseverance, godliness; and to godliness, brotherly kindness; and to brotherly kindness, love. For if you possess these qualities in increasing measure, they will keep you from being ineffective and unproductive in your knowledge of our Lord Jesus Christ. But if anyone does not have them, he is nearsighted and blind, and has forgotten that he has been cleansed from his past sins. Therefore, my brothers, be all the more eager to make your calling and election sure. For if you do these things you will never fall, and you will receive a rich welcome into the eternal kingdom of our Lord and Savior Jesus Christ." (2 Peter 1:5-11)

Just exactly how do we become excellent Christians? We develop excellency. Peter says that we are to "make every effort." Being an excellent Christian does not happen effortlessly. We do not have to work for our salvation, for our salvation is a gift. But living the excellent Christian lifestyle takes effort on our part. Why? Because the devil doesn't like excellent Christians, and you can bet that he will throw up some resistance that you will have to make an effort to stand against or push aside or climb over.

Developing excellency in our Christian walk is a progression. Peter gives us the recipe here. He says start with faith. All of us do. We receive Christ by grace through faith. Then we add a measure of goodness. Not too hard so far. Most of us by nature want to be "good" people. Put in plenty of knowledge. Okay, that means Bible study, doesn't it? That's going to take a little more effort and time on my part. But if we are going to be excellent Christians, knowledge is a very important ingredient. What's next? Add a little self-control. That means facing temptation head on. You're standing there face to face with that pan of brownies. Or, you're browsing through the video store, and the only movies that look the least bit interesting are the ones you "know" (through His divine nature) that you shouldn' t watch. Or, maybe someone just told you a fascinating piece of "news" about someone else that is not complimentary, and you start making a list in your mind of who you are going to call. These are times to "make every effort" to develop self-control in our lives. There are many other forms of temptation. You <u>and</u> the enemy know your own personal weaknesses.   If we are successful in developing a pattern of self-controlled choices, then we are adding perseverance to our lifestyle. Perseverance means continuing on or sticking with it. One of the most valuable scriptures we can cling to in the face of trials or temptations is **1 Cor. 10:13 "But when you are tempted, He will also provide a way out so that you can stand up under it."** If we recognize that, each new obstacle becomes easier and perseverance becomes a part of our character. Speaking of character, if we have worked everything into our lifestyle we' ve mentioned so far, godliness is sure to follow. And godliness doesn' t mean we are gods; it just means we start behaving in ways that are pleasing to God. Next, taking care of and loving each other becomes a constant in our make-up. Why? It' s because we' ve developed a lifestyle that no longer revolves around "self." We are starting to develop the qualities of Jesus.

So Peter says here that if we develop Christ-like qualities in our lives in increasing measure that they will keep us from being ineffective and unproductive, which must mean that we will be effective and productive. And that is how God wants us to live and how we should want to live for God. But…here' s a "but"…if we <u>don' t</u> develop these qualities, then we are nearsighted and blind and we must have forgotten what the Lord has done for us. So, self-centeredness or lack of effort or the neglect of God in our lives causes us to lose our focus, sometimes even to the point of spiritual blindness. How many of us have ever told ourselves so many times that a particular sin in our lives wasn' t "that" bad and before long we didn' t even see it as sin anymore? All because we just got lazy or began to take God for granted. **"You have forsaken your first love." (Rev. 2:4)**

Peter then advises us to "be all the more eager" to make our calling and election sure. Not that we have to do these things <u>for</u> our salvation, but we <u>have to </u>(have an urgent desire) do these things

<u>because</u> of our salvation. And when we do, our lives here on earth will be richer and our welcome into heaven will also be richer.

Does the <u>way</u> you live identify for <u>whom</u> you live? Do you consider yourself to be a "good enough" Christian, or are you willing to follow the recipe to become the "excellent" Christian God wants you to be?

Prayer thought: Lord, thank You for Your Word and for the instructions for living that it contains. Holy Spirit, You have shown me the ingredients necessary in my life to walk in excellence. My desire, Lord, is to be effective and productive for Your kingdom because of the effectiveness of Jesus' blood that produced new life for me. Lord, let these qualities be so stirred and blended in my life that the excellent Christian You see within me becomes the excellent Christian that others see in my life.

Works Every Time

"Now when Daniel learned that the decree had been published, he went home to his upstairs room where the windows opened toward Jerusalem. Three times a day he got down on his knees and prayed, giving thanks to his God, just as he had done before." (Daniel 6:10)

Have you ever placed pressure on the brake pedal of your car and suddenly felt your foot and the pedal pressed against the floor board, while your vehicle continued moving at the same rate of speed? An immediate sense of panic results because of the unexpected. Obviously, we expect that when we put our foot on the brake in our car that the car is going to slow down and eventually stop. Do we expect that to happen 50% of the time, or maybe 75%? No, we expect it to happen every time. Why? Because if the brakes fail to work just one time, we may very well be involved in a serious accident. If that does happen and we survive, we immediately take the car to get the brakes fixed, because nothing less than 100% consistency is acceptable to us. Inconsistency could be very dangerous.

I suppose it's very easy to see where we are going with this. We've talked earlier about the need for us to strive to become excellent Christians. And one of the ways we do that is by becoming consistent in our behavior. There is certain behavior that you expect from your pastor or Sunday School teacher and if they deviate from that you might say something like, "I really never expected that from them." Then you would be in confusion about the validity of the things that they preach or teach. And I singled out church leaders, but the same principle applies to each of us. When we walk out of the church and into the world wearing the label "Christian" before men, then we'd better be willing to back it up with consistent Christian behavior. After all, it's not the twenty people in our Sunday School class or the few hundred in our church congregation that we have to convince that we love Jesus and that He has made a difference in our life. It is those in the world. And you cannot do that with words alone. And you cannot do it by simply wearing a Christian T-shirt. In fact, it can do more harm than good. If the world sees you wearing a shirt that says, "God rules," or "Talk is cheap. If you're going to talk the talk, you have to walk the walk," and they can clearly see by your daily, consistent lifestyle that He doesn't rule in your life and you don't walk what you talk, you can destroy your opportunity to introduce them to Jesus.

The bottom line is that we have to develop consistent Christian behavior in our lives, so that people who are looking for answers know what to expect. Why? Just like our car's brakes, it could be a life or death matter for them. A fifty-percent consistency ratio is not acceptable.

Prayer thought: Lord, just as Daniel was consistent in his walk with You, let me daily show the world that I belong to You, not just by my words, but by every behavior choice that I make. Because of Daniel's consistent behavior, a king's heart was changed. As a follower of Christ, You have given me Your name to display to the world. Anything less than 100 % consistency to that name is unacceptable to me. When I fail, Lord, immediately get me into the "shop" to make the necessary corrections in my life. Lives are depending on my consistency.

Solid Oak Christians

"The man of integrity walks securely, but he who takes the crooked path will be found out." (Proverbs 10:9)

Sometimes things aren't always what they seem. Think about the terms "veneer" and "gold plating" as they relate to material items. Furniture or jewelry treated in these ways are meant to be imitations of the real things. Veneered furniture is made to look like real oak or mahogany, but if you pop it off, you'll find that it is not oak all the way through. Gold-plated jewelry or zircons have a similar appearance to genuine gold or diamonds, but they in no way have the same value.

Why are we talking about imitations? Have you ever sat next to somebody in church who gave a really good impression of someone who loved, trusted, and wanted to please the Lord? I mean they had on the church smile all through the service. When the preacher said, "Turn to Obadiah," they turned right there without even looking in the index. But come Monday morning, when the tests came, when the boss announced there were going to be some layoffs, or when the guys in the shop started telling them about their adventuresome weekend, the veneer came off. The trust they said they had in God to meet their needs on Sunday must have washed off in the shower. The love they said they had for the Lord and their desire to please Him didn't quite go all the way through to the second layer of their heart. And I'm speaking about these people in the third person, the "other guy," because surely none of us have ever been guilty of wearing our Christianity in layers. Surely all of our behavior, if examined under the jeweler's eye, would show us to be Christ-like all the way through to the bone.

Maybe not? Well, if not, then we'd better be thinking about it, because whether we like it or not, we are under somebody's microscope all the time. In fact, there may be people in the world who may set us up just to see if we'll fail. And if that's the case, there's no sense in getting upset with them, because it may be that

God is allowing them to test our integrity. Integrity is the key word for today. Integrity is the stuff we're made of. It's not the paint on the outside. It's the substance of our lives. I saw a quote on a church board once that read, "Your reputation is what man thinks you to be. Your character is what God knows you to be." If we are people of strong character and godly integrity, it will follow us out of the church house and into our everyday lives. And it is imperative for the kingdom that it does follow us in order for God to use us to convince other people that our faith is real. Ask yourself this question: "Am I a solid oak Christian? Or, is it only applied to my surface layer?"

Prayer thought: Dear Lord, forgive me for the times when my integrity has been less than what it should be. I don't want to be a surface Christian. I want to be valuable in Your kingdom. I want my love and desire for You to show as pure and genuine under the world's microscope as well as under Yours, Father. Purify me, Lord, from the inside out.

What's Your Excuse?

"The wrath of God is being revealed from heaven against all the godlessness and wickedness of men who suppress the truth by their wickedness, since what may be known about God is plain to them, because God has made it plain to them. For since the creation of the world God's invisible qualities—his eternal power and divine nature-have been clearly seen, being understood from what has been made, so that men are without excuse." (Romans 1:18-20)

God cannot be overlooked. God cannot be shut out. God cannot be ignored. God cannot be denied. Paul talks about the wrath of God in this passage. The wrath of God exists. We do not like to talk about it. We like to think about God only as loving and merciful. But the truth is that because God is loving and merciful, His wrath against sin has to be shown. Sin is an eternal death agent. In addition to the harm it brings to us, it dishonors God. God has to expose sin for what it is and what it brings upon His people. And sometimes that has to be done emphatically. I think of it this way. If one of my teenagers were to get arrested for DUI, I wouldn't stop loving that child, but you can rest assured that the wrath of Mom would come down on him or her. Why? Because the next time I might be going to the hospital to identify the body. Most of us who are parents understand the necessity of "emphatic discipline," so we should understand the necessity of the wrath of God in disciplining us. Verse 18 says truth is suppressed by wickedness. That is so true. Wickedness, or sin, left unconfronted or unexposed hides the truth about its destruction. Thank goodness God reveals Himself to us in His wrath.

God also reveals Himself to us in His creation. Few people can look at the complex nature of the earth, the creatures of the earth, the natural phenomenon of the earth, the human body, etc., and not marvel at the Creator. Paul says there is much evidence of an Almighty God here, so man is without excuse in acknowledging His existence. Acknowledging His existence is the first step. Acknowledging our need for Him and His salvation is the next.

Prayer thought: Father, thank You for being a loving parent to me. Thank You for the times of discipline in my life that revealed to me the path of destruction I was on. Thank You for showing Yourself to me in such I way that I recognized Your holiness and my sinful condition. And, thank You that You left me no excuse to remain there.

Can I Handle Abundance?

"Then the Lord said to Satan, 'Have you considered my servant Job? There is no one on earth like him; he is blameless and upright, a man who fears God and shuns evil.'" (Job 1:8)

Satan and a group of angels had a face-to-face encounter with God. God asked Satan where he had been, and he replied, "Roaming back and forth in the earth." The Lord inquired of Satan if he had taken notice of his righteous servant Job while he was roaming. The Lord was well pleased with the character of Job. God Himself called Job "blameless and upright." Now, that doesn't mean that he was sinless. It just meant that his character was consistent with his confessed faith.

Job had been very well blessed. He was well respected. He had a nice family, a very large herd of animals, and many servants. Verse 3 in Job 1 says, **"He was the greatest man among all the people of the East."** It was easy to take notice of Job because he was very noteworthy. Although in reading the book of Job, we most often take note of how Job remained faithful in the bad times, we should also take note that immense wealth did not taint him. For some people, overabundance drives away their need for God and causes them to lose the humility necessary to come to God. Jesus talked about the difficulty of the rich man to enter the kingdom of heaven. (**Matthew 19:23-24**) Jesus didn't say that it was impossible for them to enter, just difficult. His observation of sinful human nature showed a tendency of the wealthy to worship their wealth, as was the case with the rich, young ruler.

But there are those who can handle abundance, and Job was one of them. The apostle Paul mentions in Philippians 4:11-12 the principle of <u>learning</u> to be content in our circumstances. In other words, we should not let our circumstances dictate the person we are, but in all of our circumstances be content and consistent. Sometimes we question God as to why we don't have the blessings that others have. Maybe God knows that we couldn't handle it. Maybe He knows that our focus would change, or that we would exchange our gratefulness for smugness. Perhaps our need for God would be replaced by greed. On the other hand, we do know that God is good and that He wants to bless His children, just as earthly parents want to bless their children. But He is more interested in developing our character than in increasing our bank accounts. After Job' s testing, God had proved to Satan that it was possible for man to remain steadfast in his faith. Job' s circumstances then changed, and God blessed him two-fold for everything that he had lost. God knew that Job could handle it.

How about us? How much of our thirst for God involves seeking after His hand? Are we too focused on our material needs or desires? Have we forgotten that God knows what we need and has promised to be our Supplier? There are two scriptures that come to my mind about receiving from the storehouse of God' s blessings. Psalms 37:4 says, **"Delight yourself in the Lord and He will give you the desires of your heart."** and Matthew 6:33, **"Seek ye first the kingdom of God, and all these things shall be added unto you."** Both of these scriptures start with a condition. They are conditions that attest to our character. God has to know that we can handle abundance before He releases it to us.

Prayer thought: Lord, help me not to focus on the lack or the abundance in my life. Let me look to your servant Job as an example of unchanging spiritual integrity. Bring me to that place where my heart is consumed with seeking after You, delighting myself in You, and not chasing after the things of this world. I'm thankful that You are the perfect Father who understands my spiritual development and who releases to me only those things that You know I can handle.

Can I Handle Loss?

"His wife said to him, 'Are you still holding on to your integrity? Curse God and die!' He replied, 'You are talking like a foolish woman. Shall we accept good from God, and not trouble?' In all of this Job did not sin in what he said." (Job 2:9-11)

In reading the account of Job up to the point of our scripture reference today, you will see that Job's life had been dramatically changed from the first five verses. He had experienced the loss of his herds, his servants, and his children. This was much more than the majority of us could bear. The message brought by the last messenger was a crushing blow. He had not lost one child, but all of his children. How did he respond?

Verse 20 says, **"At this point Job got up and tore his robe and shaved his head. Then he fell to the ground in worship..."** I'm not sure I could have responded in that way at that moment, but I'm thankful for Job's example of the strength of his relationship with God. I'm sure at this point Job was wondering why God was allowing these things to happen. We are all like that. There is not a one of us who hasn't either experienced, witnessed, heard or read about very bad things that have happened to very good people. And we've all tried to understand why God allowed them to happen. It's all right for us to ask God "why," because if He allowed it to happen, He allowed it for a reason. But He very well may not choose to reveal that purpose to us right then, and that's where our faith and our integrity must take over.

Although I'm sure the pain of Job's suffering saddened God, the prayer of Job's heart in verse 21 of chapter 1 must have pleased Him. Satan's next attack came against Job's body as he infected him with painful sores from head to toe. Even in this, Job remained faithful to his God. In our focal verse for today, we read that his wife incited him against God, yet his reply revealed his heart.

Then along came his "friends" digging through his closets, trying to find some hidden sin that they could use to satisfy their questioning minds and lack of faith. Job replied to Eliphaz, ***"But now be so kind as to look at me. Would I lie to your face? Relent, do not be unjust; reconsider, for my integrity is at stake."*** All he had left that he could call his own was his character, his integrity. Chapter 27 is an outpouring of Job's heart, a beautiful poetic tribute to God. Job shows us an example of integrity that is unequaled in human comparison, until the most perfect example in Jesus Christ. Yes, there were other wonderful children of God who showed us great instances of integrity, but none who were put through such a thorough battery of testing.

What about the testings in our lives? Have you experienced them? If not, gear up, because they will be coming. Satan is still roaming about the earth like a lion, seeking whom he may devour. Chipping away at our veneer through life's circumstances is one of his specialties. If he can show the world a crack in our integrity, even though he can't keep us out of heaven, he very well may use our compromised faith to keep someone else out. Decide now how you're going to respond to bad circumstances. Reconcile yourself to the fact that there will be times of suffering in your life and it's not your job to figure out why. If it has been brought on as a direct consequence to a sin choice in your life, the Holy Spirit will be glad to point that out to you. If it has been brought on through God's permissive will as a form of testing or purifying of your faith or for the purpose of pointing someone else to Him, He may keep silent and not tell you. He can do that. He's God. It's your job to know that God is in control, knows what you're going through and will never leave you comfortless. In the case of Job, the end of the story tells how Satan got tired of getting nowhere and left him alone. God began to bless Job and bless Job and bless Job. He gave him twice as much as he had lost. Job's integrity stood firm. Will yours?

Prayer thought: Heavenly Father, Your Word says that in this world we will experience trials and tribulations. Jesus, right now I am deciding to stand firm in my faith when the storms hit. You are my Anchor. Help me to remember what Job endured and how his character stood the test. Let every test in my life be a source of strengthening of my character.

I Can Do This!

"His divine power has given us everything we need for life and godliness through our knowledge of Him who called us by His own glory and goodness. Through these He has given us His very great and precious promises, so that through them you may participate in the divine nature and escape the corruption in the world caused by evil desires." (2 Peter 1:2-4)

How many of you feel all the time that you have an abundant life full of godliness? Well, if we don't, it's our own fault, not God's. Peter says here *"…His divine power has given us everything we need for life and godliness through our knowledge of Him who called us by His own glory and goodness."* We can do this. We can be excellent Christians. Do we accomplish this through our own power? No. And if you feel as if you can't be an excellent Christian, it's because you've been trying in your own power and have failed repeatedly, and so now you've settled for "good enough." If He lives in us, we have "knowledge of Him." And it is the knowledge of Him and His nature that should guide our lifestyle. Peter stressed the fact that knowledge of God and His nature is attainable through our personal relationship with His Son. Unfortunately, too many times we ignore the knowledge of His nature in our decisions and submit to our old nature. And it's not because we didn't "know" the better decision (His decision); it's because we chose to do something else. And you can be sure that if you have any type of relationship with Him at all, God will be right back in your heart reminding you that you "knew" better. It's called conviction.

There's a wonderful promise in verse 4. *"Through these (His own glory and goodness) He has given us His very great and <u>precious</u> promises, so that through them you may <u>participate</u> in the divine nature and <u>escape</u> the corruption in the world caused by evil desires."* We don't have to sin. We have within us the knowledge of God, and we have been given the privilege of participating in His nature. He has given us all we will ever need to make right decisions. He has given us His very own nature. Peter says we are all allowed to participate in the divine nature of God. He works through us. It is His divine nature that shows forth in our lives. He does not bestow our own divinity on us. He allows us to participate in His. Are we participating fully? Or partially? Or maybe not at all.

Prayer thought: Father, help me not to fall into the trap of accepting my shortcomings that result in sin as "normal" or "only human." Jesus, I know better. You provided the example of excellence that I am to strive for. You have given me everything I need to escape temptation by allowing me to participate in Your divine nature. Increase my knowledge of You, Lord, so that I might constantly strive to become more like You.

Is My Life a Living Sacrifice?

"Therefore, I urge you, brothers, in view of God's mercy, to offer your bodies as living sacrifices, holy and pleasing to God—this is your spiritual act of worship. Do not conform any longer to the pattern of this world, but be transformed by the renewing of your mind. Then you will be able to test and approve what God's will is—his good, pleasing, and perfect will." (Romans 12:1-2)

My Bible has boldface subtitles above sections of scripture for easier identification of the topic discussed there. Above this passage of scripture it reads "Living Sacrifices." What does it mean to sacrifice? Think of things or areas of your life where you have sacrificed for someone else. Now, think of persons who have sacrificed for you. Do you resent the sacrifices you made? Are you appreciative of the sacrifices made for you? So often our attitude toward our sacrifices are colored by the attitude of the person we are sacrificing for. How many of you parents have ever felt as if the more you do for your children the more they expect, and that they really don't seem to appreciate it anyway? Of course, that is not always the case, but sometimes those thoughts do cross our minds. And my children could tell you that those sentiments sometimes did more than cross my mind as they came out of my mouth on occasion as part of my mini-sermons on high-stress days. As humans, we have a tendency to want people to recognize our sacrifices for them and to praise us for them. It somehow takes the edge off the sacrifice. And how many times have we, after having our sacrifices ignored, responded with, "Well, we'll just see if I ever do anything for them anymore!"?

But in the realm of sacrifices, our acts can't hold a candle to the supreme sacrifice of our Lord for us. And it is in appreciation for His sacrifice that Paul urges us here to offer ourselves and our bodies as "living sacrifices" to Him and for Him, that we might please the One who demonstrated mercy on us. The giving of ourselves to Christ should be a daily gift, sacrificing our own will for His. Paul says this act of giving of ourselves becomes an act of worship for us toward our Savior.

How do we become living sacrifices? Paul tells us in verse 2. ***"Be not conformed to this world, but transformed by the renewing of your mind."*** What does it mean to conform to the world? It means that we accept their standards for living instead of God's standards. For example, we conform to the world's standards for our entertainment, in our speech, morality, honesty, integrity, etc. The movie rating system is a perfect example of conformity. As viewers we are given options of acceptability as defined by the movie industry. We all know that they have labeled "G" movies for general audiences. "PG" means parental guidance—which takes the responsibility off the producers and places it on the parents. This movie, they say, is all right for you to watch, but it's your decision as to whether or not you want your child to see it. "PG-13" means the language may be a little rough, or there may be a few violent scenes or subtle sexual references, but, hey, kids 13 or over should be able to handle it. "R" means that people who have not reached the "adult maturity level" of 17 should not see this movie. I suppose their thinking is that by thirteen or seventeen, they've probably already heard, seen, or read all this stuff anyway…so why not? And most Americans, including large numbers of the Christian population, have bought into that. We've conformed. Actually, having ratings is better than not having ratings, and it is a parent's responsibility to monitor his or her child's intake of garbage. But, we have a responsibility to our Lord and Savior to monitor our own.

The key word in verse 2 is "transformed." God is more interested in <u>changing</u> us than He is in keeping us locked under a bunch of rules. But in order for Him to change us, or transform us, we need to remember that He "sanctified" us, or pulled us away from the rest of the world. When we run back to it, slip back into it, or ease back into it, we are conforming to it. We have to make daily willful decisions not to allow that to happen.

Prayer thought: Lord, transform me. Keep my mind so focused on You that the deceptions of the world cannot divert my attention from You. Lord, as I begin to sacrifice more and more of my own desires for Your desires, the transformation will take place, even to the point where they no longer seem like sacrifices. Renew my mind. Help me to think as You think and not as the rest of the world thinks.

I'm Not There, But I'm On My Way

"And we, who with unveiled faces all reflect the Lord's glory, are being transformed into His likeness with ever-increasing glory, which comes from the Lord, who is the Spirit." (2 Corinthians 3:18)

As I taught Sunday School, there were some spiritual similarities with the people inside my classroom. We were all members of the same class within the same denomination. We all had the same pastor and heard the same sermons each week. We all had the same Sunday School book and were able to prepare for the next week's lesson. However, as I prepared to teach, I wrote each lesson in complete form, (not in outline form) in order that I might share it with people who had requested copies who were not in my Sunday morning class. And some of them did not share the same denominational similarities. My goal as a teacher was to share Jesus Christ, the offering of salvation through the cross, and the power for victorious Christian living through His resurrection and through personal relationship with Him.

The confession or acknowledgment that we are sinners, the decision to repent and ask Jesus to forgive us, save us, and change us is something that we all agree on as the first step in our new relationship with our personal Savior. But after that, each of us begins a spiritual growth and learning process that is individualized and affected by several factors.
Some of them are:

- How much time we spend with Him and how much time we spend "in the world."

- How and what we pray for. Are we spending more time praying "Lord, help me and bless me," or "Lord, teach me and change me"?

- How attentive we are to the promptings of the Holy Spirit, or "conviction."

- How much of His love we are willing to receive and then release to those who don't know Him.

- How much of the world's ways we are willing to accept and how much we are rejecting.

- How satisfied we are with where we are and how hungry we are for more of God in our lives.

These are just a few things that can accelerate or stifle spiritual growth in a person. But, my point is that all of us grow at different rates of speed, although this scripture tells us that it should be "ever-increasing," God deals with us on individual levels in our growth, just as He had to deal with us individually about our need for salvation. So just because He has taken me through a certain area of conviction and house cleaning in my life, doesn't mean that He is working in the same room in your life. But we are to be there for one another to encourage and strengthen each other in whatever stage we're going through, and we are to avoid being judgmental and critical of someone who may not be at the same place we are. We also need to be aware of the fact that those who are searching for answers in certain areas may be looking at our lives. Our life-style needs to be consistent with the words we speak and the Word of God. We may be able to save someone else from making some of the same mistakes we made, but then again they may just have to make some themselves in order for God to teach them and change them. But one thing we have to be continually on guard about is that we do not become a stumbling block to someone else's spiritual growth. Concentrate on your own spiritual growth and not the lack of it in someone else.

Prayer thought: Holy Spirit, I thank You that You are in the process of changing me from glory to glory. Lord, I know there is need for much improvement in my life and many more miles to travel on my spiritual journey, but I thank You for the distance that You have brought me. Let each day bring me one step closer to Your likeness.

Am I Walking in Wisdom?

"Now all has been heard; here is the conclusion of the matter: Fear God and keep his commandments, for this is the whole duty of man. For God will bring every deed into judgment, including every hidden thing, whether it is good or evil." (Ecclesiastes 12:13-14)

"The fear of the Lord is the beginning of knowledge, but fools despise wisdom and discipline." (Proverbs 1:7)

If you will read back in 1 Kings 3 you will see that the Lord appeared to Solomon in a dream and instructed Solomon to ask for whatever he wanted from God. Solomon asked for a discerning heart and wisdom. And the Lord was pleased with that request and said to him, *"I will do what you have asked. I will give you a wise and discerning heart, so that there will never have been anyone like you, nor will there ever be." (1 Kings 3:12)*

God also told Solomon that "if" he would walk in His ways and obey His statutes and commands, that He would give him a long life. That tells me that just because we are wise and understand what is right and what is wrong, that there is always the possibility that we may not <u>choose</u> to make the wise choice. Solomon didn' t. His discernment did not leave him; the world overtook him. In our first scripture passage today we hear Solomon "coming back to his senses," *"Now all has been heard; here is the conclusion of the matter…"* How many of us have ever said to ourselves after we have made a poor choice or a series of poor choices, "Why did I do that? I knew better than that. That was really stupid"? The good news about these verses is that we are jolted back to reality.

The consequences of poor choices, or sin, bring hurt into our lives for several reasons. Let' s look at some of them. For starters, sin choices are a result of our listening to the lies of the devil instead of to the truth of God' s Word. And His Word tells us that Satan purposes to steal, kill, and destroy. (John 10:10) So, if we are listening to him, that is what we should expect. Also, the fear of God, or the reverence or acknowledgment of His authority over our lives will become more evident when we choose to disobey Him. I don' t know about you, but when I was a child and especially an adolescent, the fear of displeasing my parents and facing their judgment kept me from making a lot of wrong choices. But when I did, the acknowledgment of their authority over my life was quickly reestablished. The consequences of sin also bring hurt into our lives so that God can expose sin for the destructive force that it is. Small children can be told over and over not to touch the stove, but once those fingers are burned and they experience the pain, they then understand what "hot" means. And, hopefully, the pain of our sin choices causes us to <u>learn</u> from our mistakes and to start looking to God for our answers before we make choices. ***"The fear of the Lord is the beginning of knowledge, but fools despise wisdom and discipline."***

Prayer thought: Lord, forgive me when I walk in foolishness instead of wisdom. As hard as this is to pray, O God, I ask that the consequences of my sin be severe enough to keep me from the greater harm that comes from continued disobedience.

Am I Chasing the Wind?

"I denied myself nothing my eyes desired; I refused my heart no pleasure. My heart took delight in all my work, and this was the reward for all my labor. Yet when I surveyed all that my hands had done and what I had toiled to achieve, everything was meaningless, a chasing after the wind; nothing was gained under the sun. (Ecclesiastes 2:10-11)

Solomon is sharing his heart in these scriptures. He is talking of his search for meaning in life in the ways of the world apart from God and how utterly meaningless those avenues of his search were. What were some of them? Wisdom, as attained by man through his own efforts. We might refer to it today as education. Pleasure. Possessions. Work or careers. Religion. Relationships. Solomon tried it all, and in it all he kept referring to his search as "meaningless, chasing after the wind," I don' t know about you, but there have been lots of times in my life when I was knee deep in relationships or projects or pleasure-seeking that I thought were going to make me happy, but found out that the happiness they brought was soon gone. And to be honest, I found out that happiness is usually fleeting, brought about by temporary, outside circumstances. And I also learned the things that make us "happy" are continually changing. When I was a child, sometimes I would receive birthday cards with five or maybe ten dimes taped inside. Those were happy days! I immediately planned a trip to the "dime store," a local department store with aisles of toys and candy in that price range. Needless to say, those days are gone and so is that avenue for happiness in my life. And then there was adolescence! That prom dress, that boyfriend, that car, that grade in algebra, winning the big basketball game…those were the things that would make me happy! And they did, for a little while. And we could probably all go on with these types of scene pictures of our search for happiness through each stage of our lives. And if we stop and think about it for a moment, we probably will begin to realize that we don' t have to go back that far. More than likely the things that make us happy this year or even this month are not the same things that made us happy last year or last month.

Circumstances are constantly changing in our lives. And if we are depending on our circumstances for our happiness, we are going to be living on a perpetual roller coaster. And the longer we live our lives without Christ, the more chasing after the wind we will become involved in. Why? Because of the unexplained emptiness in our spirit that we are trying to fill. And Satan will disguise many sin options for us as the perfect filler of that void. Yet most of us could testify that none of those things brought us lasting happiness; in fact, sometimes they brought major heartache and destruction. What we need to learn is that when searching for meaning in life, it's not temporary happiness that we should be searching for, but eternal "joy." A "joy" that wells up from the <u>inside</u> of us in the midst of, or in spite of, what's happening on the outside. It is that joy that comes from our relationship with the "Joy-giver." True meaning to life comes when and only when we recognize and understand who God is and what He has done for us. It comes when we trust Him to save us and to help us walk in victory while on this earth. It comes when we learn to follow Him in obedience and service. True life-changing, unshakable, unexplainable joy comes from being involved in a true, loving, lasting, personal relationship with the Lord. And you will no longer be chasing after the wind!

Prayer thought: Lord, how blinded by the world I was! Thank You for showing me the difference between temporary happiness and true joy. Jesus, give me discerning eyes to see others that you have put in my path who are searching in the wrong places for happiness. And give me the words, Oh God, to point them in the right direction.

How's Your Spiritual Report Card?

"My son, if you accept my words and store up my commands within you, turning your ear to wisdom and applying your heart to understanding, and if you call out for insight and cry aloud for understanding, and if you look for it as silver and search for it as hidden treasure, then you will understand the fear of the Lord and find the knowledge of God. For the Lord gives wisdom, and from his mouth come knowledge and understanding. He holds victory in store for the upright, He is a shield to those whose walk is blameless, for He guards the course of the just and protects the way of His faithful ones. (Proverbs 2:1-8)

During my years as youth leader, I would get numerous requests for prayer concerning school and grades. As the semesters were nearing an end, one that always caused a reaction from me was, "Debbie, please pray for my report card." I would usually say, "It's a little late for that now. But we can begin to pray now for more effort and discipline in your study habits for next semester." That wasn't exactly what teenagers wanted to hear. Good report cards are a direct result of good effort.

Olympic athletes train for years for their specific events. Their training regimens are strict and consistent. Many hours are spent in the gym or on the track toning and stretching muscles, developing endurance and strength. They are also mindful of their bodies' needs as they discipline themselves in the areas of diet and rest. While they are in training, their entire lives revolve around preparing for the days of the competition. It would be silly for those of us who enjoy watching the Olympics to think that we could decide a day or two before the games that we could grab a pair of tennis shoes, drive to the Olympic game site and enter a race, expecting to win. We know that would be ridiculous because we have not put forth the effort that it takes to make that dream come true.

Neither can we expect to receive the wonderful benefits or blessings from God available to us starting in verse 5 of our passage today, without putting forth the effort involved in verses 1-4. What are the actions God calls us to be involved in that we might receive more of Him, His wisdom, His blessings, and His character? A quick review above would show us that we need to accept His words, store up His commands within us, listen to Him for wisdom, apply what we've learned, call out for insight, cry aloud for understanding, and look for and search for it as if it were hidden treasure. All of that involves a committed and devoted life to study, application, and testing. It's like enrolling in the College of Spiritual Growth on the eternal plan. But if we study hard and apply what we learn in His word to our lives, then He is able to give us (vv. 5-8) understanding, knowledge, His wisdom, victory, guidance and protection. I don't know that I have all A's in these subjects, but I'm going to keep studying and stretching to get there.

Prayer thought: Father, birth in me a desire to excel in spiritual growth. Holy Spirit, remind me of the necessity of discipline in my Bible study, in my prayer time, and in the areas of ministry application. I purpose, Lord, to put forth the effort necessary to improve my spiritual report card.

All Means All, Not Some

"Trust in the Lord with all your heart and lean not on your own understanding; in all your ways acknowledge Him, and He will make your paths straight." (Proverbs 3:5-6)

This is one of those verses that is good to commit to memory. ***"Trust in the Lord with all your heart."*** So many times in the Bible we have clear instruction that God wants "all" of us. Jesus said the greatest commandment was ***"Love the Lord thy God with all thy heart, with <u>all</u> thy strength, with <u>all</u> thy might, and with <u>all</u> thy soul."*** Today's focal verse tells us that our trust in Him must be with all our heart. Jesus' words tell us that God is looking for 24-7 Christians (24 hours a day, 7 days a week). We don't always do that. Some of us are content being part-time Christians. But if we want "all" of what God has and wants for our lives, then we have to be willing to give Him "all" of us. When we say, "I give you my life, Lord," we should mean our whole lives. Yet sometimes, we want to hold on to certain areas. All means all, not some, not even most.

The next part of this verse says, ***"...and lean not on your own understanding."*** A lot of us think we are smart enough to figure things out on our own. Extremely logical or analytical people need to have a logical path to follow or a logical explanation for a result. How many of you can testify that sometimes God can veer away from the logical? And He does that to move us away from our own understanding and cause us to walk in faith and to trust Him. There are a few other verses in Proverbs that talk about the folly of getting too wrapped up in our own understanding of things. *(Proverbs 3:7, 12:15, 16:25)* Verse 6 then says we are to acknowledge Him in how many of our ways? <u>All</u> our ways. That means the big things and the little things. It also means the hard things and the easy things, the good things and the bad things. Life is just one big series of circumstances, choices, and decisions that we have to make on a daily basis. Our God is a daily God, not a weekly God. He wants to run our everyday life. Some of you may think back (or ahead) to the times when you could not wait until your parents no longer had control of your life. Maybe those feelings of being "in control" of your own life keep you from willingly giving God complete authority in your life now. But I've found that the areas of my life that I let Him control run a lot smoother and with a lot less stress and pressure than those I try to handle on my own. If I give Him control and acknowledge Him in all my ways, then He will make my pathway straight. A straight path is a lot easier to walk than a crooked one.

Prayer thought: Show me, O God, those areas of my life that I have not freely given to You. Lord, You want to give me wisdom in my decisions, victory in my circumstances, and peace during my trials. You want to be in control so that You might be glorified and that I might be protected from myself. Help me to understand my need to trade in my independence for total dependence on You.

Loose Lips and Wagging Tongues

"If anyone considers himself religious and yet does not keep a tight rein on his tongue, he deceives himself and his religion is worthless." (James 1:26)

As a parent, I can say that parents are usually very excited when their babies begin to talk. Especially with the first child, we are careful to keep our baby books handy and eager to record when they say their first word. Mothers are usually a little discouraged because most babies' first word is "DA DA." But we work with them and work with them, trying to increase their vocabulary until they reach the age of three or four. Then we wish they would be quiet for a while and stop asking so many questions.

Language is fascinating. We take our language for granted because it is such a natural part of us. One year I was reminded of the diversity of language as I watched the opening ceremonies of the Olympics and saw all the countries and nationalities represented there. Words, in whatever language we speak, are necessary for communication and education, but they are so much more than that. They can be powerful tools in the building of our relationships. Unfortunately, they can also be used as powerful destructive forces in our relationships. The media has picked up on our love to speak, to be heard, and to listen in on other people's lives as the popularity of talk shows has risen over the last few years. I think when they first began, there may have been more thought-provoking issues addressed, but as the masses became more and more interested, the topics have regressed to invoking shock as entertainment rather than thought for enlightenment. The tide has turned in the area of advertisements for political candidates from the building up of one's own credentials and qualifications to the exposure and destruction of one's opponent through "attack ads."

Words are powerful. The world uses them to satisfy self. Christians use them to edify each other and to glorify God. (Any conviction here?) It would be nice if this latter statement were 100% true. But, probably one of the strongest battles with sin that Christians have is the battle we have in the area of choosing our words. The sad fact is that most of us don' t even take the time to thoughtfully choose our words. We just open our mouths and let them fall out. As Christians, we need to be constantly aware that people are not only watching our behavior, they are listening to our conversations. Is the content of our conversation in line with our profession of faith? Think about your conversations over the last 24 hours. How much of your conversation was taken up with neutral topics such as weather, sports, news, etc.? How much was carefully chosen words of praise, encouragement, positive comments intended to edify or build up someone else or glorify God? How much was unwholesome talk, negative comments, derogatory remarks, put-downs, gossip, self-pity, venting, etc.? Be honest with yourself. You might as well be, because if you are like me, God will bring back to your mind a conversation that you had recently that may have started out neutral or edifying but turned unwholesome before it ended. During this self-examination time, we may find that we are spending too much time engaged in the wrong types of conversations. Purpose in your heart today to begin to "listen" to yourself and to allow the Holy Spirit to help you choose your words and to guide your conversations.

Prayer thought: Dear Lord, this scripture is very revealing to my heart. I do not want my religion, my witness to the lost world, to be worthless. I do not want You to be disappointed in the words that come out of my mouth. I know that even though they can be forgiven, words spoken can never be retrieved. Help me, Jesus, to be ever mindful of the power of my words and to choose them carefully.

To Speak or Not to Speak, That is the Question

"The tongue has the power of life and death, and those who love it will eat its fruit." (Proverbs 18:21) "He who guards his mouth and his tongue keeps himself from calamity." (Proverbs 21:23)

How do words have the power of life and death? Upon occasion that could mean literal life or death, for example, in the spoken verdict of a jury and the sentencing of a judge. I am also reminded of the execution of a teenage girl at Columbine High School as she was asked by her classmate, "Do you believe in God?" She spoke the word, "Yes", and seconds later she lay dead on the floor. Besides the power of words over our physical lives, though, I think this scripture most often applies to our spiritual lives. Think of a time when someone's words spoke life to you, built you up, encouraged you, pointed out something you needed, or lifted your spirits. Now, think of a time when someone's words hurt you, caused anger to rise in you, saddened you, made you feel worthless or unappreciated, depressed you, etc.

As Christians we have to understand that we are going to run into both kinds of these conversations. It is unfortunate, however, that sometimes our own words yield both life and death to others. And that becomes very confusing to those we are trying to reach for Christ. **James 3:9-10 says, "With the tongue we praise our Lord and Father, and with it we curse men, who have been made in God's likeness. Out of the same mouth come praise and cursing. My brothers this should not be."** Hypocrisy is high on Satan's top ten list for keeping people out of church. And too many of us aid him in this tactic by doing exactly what these verses say, praising God and cursing man. This should not be.

And how about the advice of our next proverb that says *"He who guards his mouth and his tongue keeps himself from calamity"?* How many of us can think of some calamity we could have avoided if we had kept our big mouth shut? On the other hand, there may have been some calamity we could have avoided if we had just opened our mouths a little sooner. Wisdom. We need to pray for and exercise wisdom. In my prayer time concerning this area, I was reminded of all the perfect choices that Jesus made, setting the example for us. He confronted the Pharisees when the time was right for confrontation. He chose words of a physical nature to teach spiritual truths to the crowds. He asked questions to answer questions that provoked inward examination of the heart. He kept silent at times when He was under direct attack. Oh, that we might choose our words as carefully as Jesus did. We can, you know, if we would just stop and pray before we speak, "Okay, Lord, what would you have me say (or not say) in this situation?" Of course, we understand that is not possible to pray before every sentence, but it is possible to pray for wisdom in our speech before we begin our day. If we would do that, we might begin to see our speech patterns or "habits" changing to conform to the examples set by Christ.

Prayer thought: Jesus, You have shown me in Your Word how my words are to be used. Help me to understand the power of my words. Help me to remember that something I say this day may bring someone a step closer to relationship with You, or drive them farther away. Lord, more than once I've felt the effect of my words on my own relationship with You. Forgive me for those times of failure, and grant me wisdom and self-control over my words this day.

Junk, Gibberish, or Juicy?

"Put away perversity from your mouth; keep corrupt talk far from your lips." (Proverbs 4:24) "A fool's lips bring him strife, and his mouth invites a beating." (Proverbs 18:6) "A gossip betrays a confidence; so avoid a man who talks too much." (Proverbs 20:19)

Well, obviously we must have a lot to learn and be mindful of in the area of our speech, as the Bible seems to have so much to say about it. Let's look more closely at the areas mentioned in these three proverbs.

The first one says we are to put away perversity and corrupt talk. I am sure that includes improper language, using God's name in vain, and ugly, off-color words we classify as foul or filthy talk. But, I think it means more than that. "Perversity" means deviating away from what is right and "corrupt" brings to mind intentional malice and deceit. Calculating words spoken only to bring about a desired result for yourself, regardless of what it does to anyone else, can be perverse and corrupt.

Solomon also talks here about the fool's lips. What does that mean? Could it mean talk that has no real meaning? Words that have nothing to back them up. Perhaps talking on a subject you know very little about. Foolish talk can get you in big trouble when you run into someone who challenges you. And the more you are challenged, the more foolish you appear.

Oh my, the next verse has that ugly "gossip" word in it. What is gossip? Most of us would agree that it is tale bearing or story spreading, behind-the-back news flashes, or "sharing" of information about someone else's life or actions. We Christians sometimes try to disguise gossip as "prayer requests." Rumors are by-products of gossip. Specifically, we think of rumors as the spreading of false statements or half-truths. And we all know what happens to gossip or rumors as they travel down the phone lines or across the lunch table or wherever they may breed. The story changes a little from one person to the next. Here's a sobering thought for Christians. People can become "addicted" to gossip, just as they can become addicted to a variety of other things. Think of the popularity of gossip papers and talk shows. Sadly, good or positive news or information does not attract as much attention nor travel as quickly as bad news or "juicy" or scandalous news. This verse says we are to avoid those people who talk too much, in particular the gossips. And we also need to avoid becoming one. Once you attain a reputation as a gossip, as this verse says, you bear the reputation for betraying confidences, and people will stop trusting you with their words.

How is your score card in these three areas? Is there any "junk" in your speech that needs to be thrown out? Are you spouting a lot of "gibberish" just to hear yourself speak or to impress others? Does "juicy" gossip appeal to you or even dominate your conversations. Ah, the wisdom of Solomon. The Lord blessed him with it in order that He might bless us with it. It's up to us to heed it.

Prayer thought: Thank You, Lord, for the wisdom found in Your Word. Thank You for the convicting nature of Holy Spirit to point out areas of weakness in my speech. Lord, I pray right now that You would remind me of specific instances where I have fallen short in this area in order that I might ask forgiveness and learn from these mistakes.

Helpful, Hopeful, and Healing

"An anxious heart weighs a man down, but a kind word cheers him up." (Proverbs 12:25) "Pleasant words are a honeycomb, sweet to the soul and healing to the bones." (Proverbs 16:24) "A gentle answer turns away wrath, but a harsh word stirs up anger."(Proverbs 15:1)

Just think how happy the Lord would be with us if we paid more attention to these verses. And, think about how much better we would feel about ourselves. And one step further, this wise advice shows us how our words can be a blessing to someone else. So, it would appear to me that developing the right vocabulary and speech patterns is a win/win situation for God, others, and ourselves.

Words of praise, words of encouragement, words of good advice, words of comfort, words of sympathy, words of understanding, positive, uplifting words, happy words...what a better world this would be if we would concentrate on this kind of speech! Verse 12:25 above says that the right word spoken at the right time has the power to lift an anxious heart. Most of us know what it is like to be anxious, concerned, or worried about something. Think of a time when you were experiencing concern over a circumstance in your life, and God sent someone to speak a word of encouragement or hope to you. The circumstance may not have changed in that instance, but the weight of it seemed to lift through the power of a few helpful words.

Pleasant words can be healing. (16:24) How important is our word "environment"? Spouses or children who may live in an environment where there are no real signs of physical abuse may be suffering daily from verbal abuse. And constant verbal abuse can manifest itself in personality disorders, self-esteem issues, physical problems, social weaknesses, etc. It can be very crippling. But, it has been proven over and over again that by removing individuals from this type of word environment and placing them in places such as safe-houses, children's homes, or foster homes where love, encouragement and hope are spoken daily into their lives, healing begins to take place. Because of the sin nature of man, it is not possible to isolate others or ourselves completely from bad "word environments." It is possible, however, for us to use our words to offer a stark contrast to that environment in order that we might be used as an instrument of healing. Pay attention to the cries for help around you. Learn to apply the sweet salve of healing words to the cuts, bruises and wounds of those around you.

And what about verse 15:1? If you have an argumentative nature and feel a strong need to debate or prove your point, or if you have a short fuse on your temper, you may need to post this verse in several highly visible places of your day. Or, better yet, memorize it and post it on your heart and ask the Holy Spirit to show it to you every time you are tempted to become involved in conversations that set off these types of responses in you. One of the hardest things we can ever learn is how to answer someone else' s anger with Christ' s gentleness. As we are learning this, we may have to learn how to take quick prayer "time outs" so that we don't explode. We need to recognize that person' s behavior as a testing of our faith. And as we begin to develop a more gentle nature, we will begin to notice a more gentle nature come over the other person. Wouldn' t you agree that is very difficult to argue with someone who refuses to return the argument? Arguments and debates are fueled by the increasing intensity of the verbal exchange. Stop throwing gas on the fire. Douse it with Living Water.

Prayer thought: Lord, I know that it is not enough just to be careful to watch what I say. That' s just a start. My heart' s desire, Jesus, is that my <u>character</u> is constantly changing to mirror Yours and that my speech begins to naturally line up with that change. Help me to examine the gospels for Your example and use my words to bring help, hope, and healing to others.

Attitudes are Revealing

"And whatever you do, whether in word or deed, do it all in the name of the Lord Jesus, giving thanks to God the Father through him." (Colossians 3:17)

In the mid-nineties I took my then junior high-aged daughter to the mall to buy school clothes, which took us to the junior department loaded with T-shirts and jeans. As I looked through the racks of T-shirts, there seemed to be an over-abundance of shirts with messages on them displaying bad attitudes. "Spoiled Brat," "Born to Be Bad," "Bad Boy Club" were just a few. I asked the sales clerk why all the T-shirts had to have such negative attitudes, and she just smiled and said it was the sign of Generation X. On the brighter side, cartoon characters were also fashionable at that time, and my daughter chose a few "Mickey" items. But, even in the cartoon arena, the "Tasmanian Devil" was the most popular.

What is "attitude" and what does it reveal about us? The dictionary defines it as "a state of mind or feeling, disposition, the way one carries oneself indicative of mood." Attitude is so important because it says so much about you. If you hate your job, you're going to have a bad attitude and it will show. If you don't like going to church, but you go because someone expects or forces you to be there, your attitude will give you away. Let's face it, everyone has a bad day once in a while, and on those days our attitudes generally worsen. The goal of Christians who love the Lord should be to exchange our attitude for the attitude of Christ. Tall order, but a worthy goal. Our title today says, "Attitudes are Revealing." Professing to be a Christian and then losing your temper in traffic, complaining about your boss or co-workers, or grumbling about things that are taking place at church sends a very confusing message to people. They may be thinking, "Are all Christians like this?" or "Is this person really a Christian?" Either way, your attitude has blown your witness. Yes, the Lord will forgive a bad attitude if we recognize it, confess and repent of it, but we may never know how much damage has been done with it. Developing a genuine Christ-like attitude in all that we do is a full-time job, but a very rewarding one.

When we receive new life in Christ, our attitudes toward everything should change to reflect the change that has taken place in us. Paul says in our verse today that whatever we do, we are to do it all in the name of the Lord Jesus. That means the mundane things and the glamorous things, the things we enjoy doing and the things we would rather not be doing (like going to the mall with a teen-ager!). As Christians, whatever we are doing, we are doing it wearing a different name, the name of the Lord Jesus. People are not only examining our behavior, but they are examining our attitude. And so is God. Paul says that we need to develop the attitude of thanksgiving in all that we do. After all, every breath we take comes from God. Every dollar we earn belongs to God. Every act of service we do for Him should be considered a privilege and not a chore. Every morning we should get up thanking God for the day and turning it over to Him. And then we might start singing a praise song. If we would all do that, it would be almost impossible to start the day with a bad attitude!

Prayer thought: Jesus, You have given me new life. Remind me of that as I get out of bed every morning. No matter what I face today, help me to monitor my attitude at all times and in all things. Help me to remember that it is not only my words and actions that reveal my relationship with You, but my attitude as well.

Why Should I Forgive Them?

"And when you stand praying, if you hold anything against anyone, forgive him, so that your Father in heaven may forgive you your sins." (Mark 11:25)

How many of us have ever been hurt by someone we love? How about someone you thought was a friend but who did or said something not very "friend-like"? How many have ever had quarrels within a family that went on for a long period of time? Well, most of us would answer "yes" to at least one of these situations. More times than not in these types of circumstances, our emotions surface very quickly. The devil can have a hay-day with our emotions.

How might we respond to these things? We might cry. We might throw ourselves a major pity party. We might get angry. We might engage in verbal combat. We might search for allies and choose up sides. We might worry. We might begin plotting revenge. We might choose just to write him or her out of our lives and forget them. We might choose to harbor bitterness. And most of us would agree that these are fairly normal responses for wronged persons. But then again, we might just dare to be different and do something totally against human nature and forgive them, go on loving them, and trust God to right our wrong. Of course, when we do that, it douses the flames on our emotions, and the chances of our being caught up in the sins that out-of-control emotions can bring is lessened. Satan loses. God wins. There is power in forgiveness. Not only does it set us free, but it also does a lot to show others the forgiving nature of our Lord, and allows Him to make something good out of a bad situation.

The question in today's title is "Why should I forgive them?" We usually follow that question up with "It was their fault," or "They hurt me too badly," or some other reason that we choose to attach to our unforgiveness. The next time you are confronted with the question, "Why should I forgive them?", picture Jesus on the cross. He had a human side. He could have very well looked toward His Father and asked, "Why should I forgive them? Look what they've done to me. I didn't do anything to them to deserve this." But He didn't say those things. He said, ***"Father, forgive them for they know not what they do."*** That statement, mixed with the blood flowing down the cross, was not only a statement for those people at that moment, but for all of us throughout the ages. It was not only a statement of pardon, but also a statement of example for us to follow.

Prayer thought: Jesus, thank You for forgiving me. I've wronged You many times, Lord, yet I have never felt You turn Your back on me. I know that Your forgiveness of my sins serves as an example for me to follow in forgiving others. In fact, Your Word says that I must do this. Whenever I'm tempted to walk in bitterness and unforgiveness, take me back to the cross. You <u>chose</u> to forgive me. No matter how difficult the devil makes it out to be, I will <u>choose</u> to forgive others.

Start With Your Family

"As Jesus was getting into the boat, the man who had been demon-possessed begged to go with him. Jesus did not let him, but said, 'Go home to your family and tell them how much the Lord has done for you, and how He has had mercy on you.'" (Mark 5:18-19)

For background today read the first seventeen verses of Mark 5. It is the story of Jesus casting the demons from the man they possessed and sending them into the herd of pigs. How do you think the former demoniac felt? What did the pig herdsmen do? How did the townspeople react? Those tending the pigs reported an event that they had seen. They were eyewitnesses. But all they could tell was what they had seen take place. The townspeople arrived, but by this time all the pigs were drowned. But then they saw for themselves the difference in the man they had known to be demon-possessed. Whether they believed the story of the eyewitnesses about the pigs or not, they could clearly see that something had changed this man. They were afraid and amazed. Because they knew something was obviously "strange" and that Jesus had been a part of it, they wanted Him to leave. The man who had been set free, however, was not afraid, and he definitely understood that it was Jesus who was responsible for freeing him. He knew by personal experience what had happened to him, and he did not want Jesus to leave without him. He did not understand that because of the change he had just experienced, spiritually speaking, Jesus would always be with him. At this point, Jesus would not let him go with Him physically because He wanted the man to go in a different direction to tell others. He was to tell others not just the story of how Jesus spoke to the demons and cast them into the pigs, but the total experience of the love and mercy of the Lord that caused Him to do this great thing specifically for him.

Jesus instructed him to go first and tell his family. Jesus knows human nature and that it is natural for us to want to share any type of good news with those whom we have the closest relationships. For instance, when we get a raise or a promotion at work, or when our child takes his first step, or when we get a new car, we don't pick up the phone book and start calling strangers. We start by sharing with those closest to us, those we know will listen and be happy for us and share in our excitement. In some instances, however, Christians may find it difficult to witness to their unsaved family members. Why is that? Maybe it's because our families, or those people closest to us, are the ones who knew the "old us" better than anyone. And sometimes they are amazed and afraid, just like the townspeople in our story above. They may think our new behavior is strange and are skeptical that it will last and of the Source. So, we shouldn't let it burst our bubble if we are initially met with some resistance from family members. On the other hand, in most family or close personal relationships, there should be a foundation of trust already established there that should cause them to believe us before they would a stranger. And sometimes after the initial shock of our conversion wears off and they begin to see that the changes in us are real and are definitely for the better, they begin to listen a little more attentively.

Jesus sent this man home to tell his family. And the man obeyed. Who in your family or close circle of influence needs to hear about Jesus and His love and mercy? Tell them your story. Let them see in your lifestyle that He has made a difference. If you love them, don't you want them to remain a part of your family in eternity?

Prayer thought: Jesus, thank You for changing my life. Thank You for making the gospel available to my family and friends. I see now that verse 19 was not just a directive to this man, but a directive to me. Help me to understand that I have the opportunity through an already established relationship to share You with them. And that it is not only an opportunity but also a responsibility.

It All Starts at Home

"The righteous man leads a blameless life; blessed are his children after him." (Proverbs 20:7)

God places us all in families, even though all families are not alike. Some may be large, while others are small. Some have a lot of money, and others struggle to survive. Some are biologically linked, and some are not. But the family, as designed by God, was meant to bond people together in intimate, caring, deep, and lasting relationships. It is to be a place where we learn to love, give and take, and obey the rules of the home. We should feel secure, comfortable and free to be ourselves there. It should be a place where our needs are met. We are supposed to learn responsibility and respect within our families. And it should be the place where we begin our spiritual training.

Now, those are some of the things that are supposed to take place in the family. Indeed if all of those things happened as God designed, this world would not be in the sad shape that it is. Satan learned very early, (in the Garden of Eden), that if he was going to have any control over people' s lives, he was going to have to start in the family. Satan is bent on destroying families because broken or improper relationships will keep us from learning how to equate loving, fulfilling, earthly relationships with the relationship God wants to have with us. And when those examples are not there, it takes longer for us to learn that there is somebody who loves us for who we are, no matter what we do, nor how many times we mess up. It takes longer for us to learn that there is somebody we can trust. It takes longer for us to learn that when we pray to our Father in heaven, that He is not a parent that is going to yell at us, hurt us, or abandon us. It takes longer for us to learn that when God says, "I'll love you forever," that forever does not mean "until you upset me, or get on my nerves, or I find somebody else."

When we learn how to make wise choices in our homes, we will begin to see the results in our families. When husbands and wives learn to treat each other with honor and respect, it teaches honor and respect as the norm in the family, and that is passed on to the next generation. And whether or not your family is typical, (if there is such a thing anymore), or if you are a single parent raising children, or a grandparent in charge, adoptive or foster parents, or any other adult authority in the home, the rules and responsibilities of role-modeling fall to you. Too often in today's society, adults do not take this responsibility seriously. The role models are too busy trying to find themselves or have their needs fulfilled that they abandon their roles in the home.

God knew what He was doing when He designed the family. Satan knew what He was doing when he set out to destroy it. Check the structure of your home. Have you had it "treated" with the blood of Jesus?

Prayer thought: Father God, as I look all around me I see the devastating effects of the destruction of the family. Lord, help us as adults in our homes to understand the responsibility we have to model godly relationships before our children. Show us plainly, O Lord, areas in our homes that need to be Satan-proofed. Future generations are counting on us.

Perfect Parenting Tips

"When I was a boy in my father's house, still tender, and an only child of my mother, he taught me and said, 'Lay hold of my words with all your heart; keep my commands and you will live. Get wisdom, get understanding; do not forget my words or swerve from them.'" (Proverbs 4:3-4)

"Train a child in the way he should go, and when he is old he will not turn from it." (Proverbs 22:6)

"Discipline your son, and he will give you peace; he will bring delight to your soul." (Proverbs 29:17)

Children are brought into this world totally dependent on the nurture and the protection of the people with whom they live. Their entire world is viewed in the confines of the home in which they dwell. They learn from the things they see, hear, and experience within those walls. It is how they view life until they are old enough to see outside of those boundaries.

Parents are teachers. Those with children cannot count on the school systems or even the church to teach values, standards, and proper behavior to the people that God has put under their charge. Sadly, however, sometimes it takes other institutions to straighten out the mistakes that parents have made in the home. Now, I'm not saying that to bring guilt and condemnation on parents who have made mistakes with their children, because we all have. The key is that we admit when we have made mistakes and try to correct them and learn from them. And sometimes you can look at homes where you know proper instruction has taken place and still see a child who rebels against what he has been taught. And if that is the case, Proverbs 22:6 is probably a favorite verse in that home.

There are three things in these verses that we need to learn as parents. 1) Teach children to love the Word of the Lord. 2) Train them in proper behavior. 3) Discipline them for correction. I am sure that as we read through the rest of the Proverbs we could find a treasure chest of parenting tips. My advice to those of you who are now parents or who will someday be parents is not to put too much stock in the parenting techniques of self-help books or child psychologists. The wisest and most tested and proven advice for parents is contained in the Word of God.

My children are all adults now, and I am very thankful for the people that they have become. But most of all I am thankful to God that He began a radical change in my life, turning my heart more toward Him and increasing my hunger for Him back many years ago when three sets of small eyes were looking to me for direction. My pastor says, "Some things are taught and some things are caught." You can teach your kids about Jesus, but they also need to see that you truly love Him.

Prayer thought: Father, what an awesome blessing our children are in our lives. Yet, what an enormous responsibility we have in raising them. We are called to be teachers and role models, providers, protectors, counselors, disciplinarians, and a variety of other things in their lives. And, Lord, sometimes we mess up. Thank You for Your grace. Lord, help us always to look to You as the example of the perfect parent. Thank You for our instruction book. I see now that _my_ relationship with You is a key factor in becoming the kind of parent that You want me to be.

Too Much Togetherness

"Wives, submit to your husbands, as is fitting to the Lord. Husbands, love your wives and do not be harsh with them. Children, obey your parents in everything, for this pleases the Lord. Fathers, do not embitter your children, or they will become discouraged." (Colossians 3:18-21)

What do we think of when we think of families? The word "family" usually has a positive connotation. We bring to mind holidays and smiling faces around a Christmas tree or a dinner table. We think of the family picture album or the family vacations. Maybe we remember those heart-to-heart talks or times of sharing in special accomplishments. Why, then, did Paul feel it necessary to give us such strong words on how to treat the members of our family? Maybe it's because that sometimes too much togetherness tends to expose all of our weaknesses as well as our strengths to each other.

I'll never forget that once when my youngest daughter was around 10 or 11 years old, she looked up at me after I had responded very badly to a minor incident and said, "Mom, how come that sometimes you are a lot nicer to other people than you are to us?" I stood there with my mouth open and the knife of conviction stuck in my heart. Until that moment, I had not even realized that I had been showing any difference. But the truth was that I did try harder to be nice to other people, and at home I let my guard down and allowed any bad moods or attitudes I might be experiencing to show up there. After all, I thought, they were my children. They knew that I loved them. So if I had a bad day at the office, and seemed a little edgy when I got home, and over-reacted to a messy kitchen or unfinished homework, they would get over it. How sad!

Attitudes are extremely important in families because we spend so much time together. The people we live with are supposed to be the people we love the most, and that love should be displayed in how we treat one another. Yet, many times, we make much greater efforts to be nice, kind, polite, and cordial to casual acquaintances or even complete strangers than we do to members of our own families. Why? Maybe it's because we take their feelings and their love for granted and don't feel the need to "impress" them with our kindness. Many homes or family relationships are destroyed because of this type of negligence. Make an effort this week to show your family how much you love them.

Prayer thought: Lord, thank You for my family. Thank You, Holy Spirit, for Your words of instruction on how we should treat one another. Help me daily, Lord, to demonstrate by my attitude toward my family how much they mean to me. And if I have an attitude failure, help me not only to ask for Your forgiveness, but theirs as well. Help me to remember that developing better family attitudes develops better families.

Pass the Salt, Please

"You are the salt of the earth. But if the salt loses its saltiness, how can it be made salty again? It is no longer good for anything, except to be thrown out and trampled by men." (Matthew 5:13)

Have you ever been in the hospital or have had some sort of medical condition that required that you be put on a bland diet? You are instructed to eat foods without seasoning or spices that might irritate your stomach or colon or whatever area they are trying to protect. It's still food and it still nourishes your body, but the flavor is absent. Mealtime becomes rather dull and less enjoyable. A lot of people look at the lives of Christians as a bland life…no spice, no flavor, not very enjoyable. If that is the case, then we need to do a better job of making our lives more appetizing to them.

The Christian life should be brimming with flavor. The salt of the gospel, salvation by grace, has to be added first and then tasted in order to be appreciated. Then our lives will be "spiced up" with things like peace, joy, love, laughter, compassion, more patience, less guilt, kindness, etc. The world (from whence we came), however, tries to add flavor to their lives, too. But they are using a different set of spices; things like unscriptural sexual practices, alcohol or drugs, crude jokes, laughter at the expense of others, gossip, selfish indulgences, etc. The problem is that these types of spices have a major tendency to back up on us, cause a lot of pain, or eventually destroy our lives. As Christians we have been made aware that these types of things are to be avoided for a healthy, happy life.

And how have we been made aware of it? Maybe because someone passed us the salt of the gospel. Once you have tasted that salt, no other seasoning or spice can ever replace it. It becomes our job then to pass it along to someone else. Pass it to those who may have had their other "spices" turn on them. Pass it to those who have yet to choose with which set of spices they want to flavor their lives. Don't let your Christian life appear bland to those seeking seasoning. Generously sprinkle the Salt in your own lifestyle and make it so appetizing to others that they begin asking you to, "Please pass the salt!"

Prayer thought: Jesus, in Your very own words, You told us that we are the salt of the earth. You expect us to live our lives in such a way that we make others hungry and thirsty for You. Lord, help us to clean out all other spices from our lives, so that we don' t pollute others or ourselves with the way we live. Put so much salt on our shelves that we just have to start using it in greater quantities and still have plenty to give away!

Preserve and Illuminate

"You are the salt of the earth. But if the salt loses its saltiness, how can it be made salty again? It is no longer good for anything except to be thrown out and trampled by men. You are the light of the world. A city on the hill cannot be hidden. Neither do people light a lamp and put it under a bowl. Instead they put it on its stand, and it gives the light to everyone in the house. In the same way, let your light shine before men, that they may see your good deeds and praise your Father in heaven." (Matthew 5:13-16)

We've talked about the use of salt as a flavoring agent, but there is another use of salt that should be addressed. Jesus used it as an example with a crowd of people who lived in a world without refrigeration and the use of salt was extremely important in the preservation of food. Not only are we called to add flavor and make the Christian life more appetizing to others, we are also called to "preserve" the earth from the corruption that life without Christ brings. Salt is a preservative. We are to be preservatives. Even though Christians are branded as uncompromising or close-minded, it is up to us to try to preserve the moral standards and values established in the Word of God, not to exalt ourselves or to put others down, but to try to save the world from destroying themselves.

As salt-sprinkling Christians, we should be vocal about God's views on abortion, pornography, alcohol and drug use, sexual relations outside of marriage, unwholesome or ungodly vocabularies, etc. What happens when we begin applying salt to some of these issues? It becomes an irritant to some people, much like applying salt to an open wound. Be ready for a reaction. Obviously, we have to watch our motives when applying salt in these instances. Our motives should not be to purposefully irritate people by placing ourselves in an exalted position of being judge and jury. We are just to add the salt of the gospel and the grains of truth as we know them and then let the Holy Spirit do the irritating. For example, if you have made it clear in your workplace by a consistently demonstrated life that you do not take the Lord's name in vain and that it bothers you when others do, then your presence in the break room or on the assembly line may become an irritant to those who do not hold that same standard in their lives.

Sometimes when an issue is controversial and you are challenged on your stand, be prepared to share from God's Word on the subject. Of course, that means you will need to have your Bible with you and know where to open it. In addition to salt, we are called to be light. When we can show others the truth as God spoke it, we allow the Holy Spirit to expose the sin in the light of His Word. Again, be careful that you are not using God's Word to win a debate so that you can declare your self-righteousness, but that you are using it as a beacon lamp for those who aren't even aware that they are in the dark. Where it goes from there depends on their reaction to the Word.

On the other hand, what happens when our lives lose their saltiness or we hide the light under a bowl? We fail to make a difference in the world, and more directly, in the individual lives in whom God has given us a position of influence. It could have eternal consequences. Preserve and illuminate.

Prayer thought: Dear Lord, forgive me for the times when I've hidden Your light from those around me. Forgive me for the times I've failed to make my stand on sin apparent for fear of being irritating. Lord, I ask You to increase my knowledge of Your Word through diligent study so that I am more able to be effective in this world as salt and light.

I Want to be in His Flock

"I am the good shepherd. I know my sheep and my sheep know me—just as the Father knows me and I know the Father—and I lay down my life for the sheep." (John 10:14-15)

Jesus identifies Himself in this section of scripture, actually beginning with verse 11, with one of the seven "I am" statements in the book of John. He says, *"I am the good shepherd."* But then He goes on in verses 12 and 13 to qualify His choice of the word "good" shepherd by contrasting it with an "ordinary" shepherd, or a mere hired hand, by declaring His supreme devotion to His sheep. In our focal verses today, Jesus talks about the personal <u>relationship</u> He has with His sheep and His willingness to lay down His life for them. Those who were present when He spoke those words saw Him fulfill them a short time later at Calvary.

Jesus used the sheep/shepherd analogy because it was easily understood in that culture at that time. Pet owners understand the relationship that develops between themselves and their pets. Your pet will respond to your voice or your movements in a much different way than it will to a stranger. And even though sheep are livestock, they still responded to their shepherd in much the same way, because of the dependence they had developed with their particular shepherd. And the "good" shepherds developed a recognition and a devotion to their own sheep. Even if their sheep were mixed in with other sheep, good shepherds could still recognize their own.

And that is exactly what Jesus is saying to us. *"I am the good shepherd. I know my sheep and my sheep know me."* Jesus knows us through and through. He knows our thoughts. He knows our weaknesses. He knows our problems, our heartaches, the things that make us happy, our abilities, and on and on. A good shepherd knows everything there is to know about his sheep. He must in order to provide for all they need. A grateful and loving sheep seeks to know His shepherd, stay close to Him, and learn the boundaries He has established. He learns to recognize the Shepherd's voice and to be obedient to His commands. This verse is just another example of the absolute necessity of having a personal relationship with Jesus Christ. It's not enough for a sheep wandering off by himself somewhere just to "believe" that "somewhere" in the world there is a shepherd watching out for him. He is going to be destroyed. How many times have you heard people who show no signs of a personal relationship with the Lord say, "Oh, I believe in God." That's not enough. You have to become a part of His flock, keep close to Him, and develop a personal relationship with the "Good Shepherd."

Prayer thought: Jesus, I was a former little lost sheep. Thank You for seeking me out and making me a part of Your flock. My prayer is that my relationship with my Shepherd becomes so deep and personal that I immediately respond to Your voice of direction and correction in order that I might enjoy Your protection and the security of being in Your presence.

The "Why" Behind My "Do"

"If anyone thinks he is something when he is nothing, he deceives himself. Each one should test their own actions. Then he can take pride in himself, without comparing himself to somebody else, for each one should carry his own load." (Gal. 6:3-5)

Before we can begin to help or encourage someone else, we have to be filled with a supply of encouragement that does not come from ourselves. If we start thinking that we are the answer to everyone's problem, or adopt the "I can fix this" philosophy, then we are deceiving ourselves. God's glory will be shared with no man.

It is very easy sometimes for someone's <u>gratitude</u> toward us to turn into an <u>attitude</u> for us. People in high profile ministries especially have to be very careful. Pastors, preachers, teachers, musicians, and church leaders often find themselves being praised for their acts of service. We like to be thanked. We like to be appreciated and told that we did a good job, or were a big help, etc. But after that, we have to continue to test our response to that gratitude and our future actions. Are we doing it to glorify God and to show others the love of Jesus that overflows in our heart, or are we doing it for the compliments or the pats on the back? We need always to ask God to purify our motives, because it is our motives for good works that will be tested at the judgment seat of Christ. If Satan can't keep us from doing good things but can corrupt our motives, he has still accomplished his goal.

God wants us to act genuinely. We must do what we do out of love. God can spot a phony and, most of the time, so can the people you are trying to help. Don't try to compare your good deeds with someone else's. You'll either get a swelled head or frustrated or jealous. Christians are not in competition with each other. You are responsible only for your own acts of obedience. God will bring the harvest. And He will reward the faithful in ways that far exceed the praise of man.

Prayer thought: Lord, only You are worthy of praise and honor and glory. Jesus, keep my motives for service pure. Protect me from the attitude of haughtiness that can come from the praise of others.

Come On, You Can Do It!

"You are witnesses, and so is God, of how holy, righteous and blameless we were among you who believed. For you know that we dealt with each of you as a father deals with his own children, encouraging, comforting and urging you to live lives worthy of God, who call you into his kingdom and glory." (1 Thessalonians 2:10-12)

Earlier in this chapter Paul told the Thessalonians how they, (Paul, Silas, and Timothy) had treated them like a mother caring for her children, and in this passage Paul says we also dealt with you as a father deals with his children. Besides the nurturing and tending to needs, we also need to be a friend that encourages, strengthens, and urges our friends to begin a stronger walk with the Lord. That means encouraging them to make better decisions—decisions that Christ would have them make in order to bless them and also to "live lives worthy of God, who calls you into his kingdom and glory." That puts a tremendous responsibility on us, then, to live our lives before them as "holy, righteous and blameless." They have to see that it is possible.

Throughout the last good many years of my life, the Lord has placed me in positions of leadership over small groups of people. I spent many years as a young adult Sunday School teacher, which, by the way, provided the impetus for this book. I am currently leading singles in our church in a weekly home Bible study. For over ten years, I poured my life into youth ministry. Leading by example is very important to me. I was very atypical as a youth leader. Most youth ministers are 25-35-year-old males, who are either part-time or full- time staff. I was about ten years older, a female, single mother, with a full-time secular job, and a volunteer. The Lord definitely had His hand on that ministry! One of the things that made it effective was that I became a mother figure to most of my teens. For the most part, they would tell me their problems and share their prayer concerns with me, but they didn' t share too many of their struggles with sin with me, because it would have been like telling their mother.

However, living in a small town, like most mothers, I found out most of it. But besides being the person who passed out hugs, birthday presents, food, and Kleenex for tears, I also had to be careful to be a standard for righteousness that they could see. They knew what decisions I was going to make in certain situations. I had to be able to encourage them and instruct them in God's standards so they could begin to make right decisions on their own. Even though they clearly knew what I approved of and what I didn't, I had to show them in God's Word where those standards came from and why they should act, react, and behave according to the character of Jesus that they were to display to the world.

Who are you encouraging to live their lives for God? Start with the person in your bathroom mirror. As you begin to consistently live by His standards, you will become an encouragement to someone who may be struggling. Even if you don't speak the words, your life will say, "Come on, you can do it!"

Prayer thought: Oh, Lord, make my life an encouragement to others. Let your Word be my standard for decision-making. And let that be apparent to those who are examining my life. I know that none of us are worthy on our own, but that we have only been made worthy through Your blood, Jesus. Help us to live our lives in gratitude for that sacrifice by walking in Your footsteps.

The Big "D"

"Finally, be strong in the Lord and in his mighty power. Put on the full armor of God so that you can take your stand against the devil's schemes. For our struggle is not against flesh and blood, but against the rulers, against the authorities, against the powers of this dark world and against the spiritual forces of evil in the heavenly realms. Therefore put on the full armor of God so that when the day of evil comes, you may be able to stand your ground, and after you have done everything, to stand." (Ephesians 6:10-13)

Everyone is familiar with the concept of team sports. They are a big part of the American way of life. Even though most of us never become professionals, many of us have participated in organized team sports, such as basketball, baseball, softball, soccer, football, swimming teams, tennis, etc. And if we haven't participated, there is certainly enough emphasis on them in high school, college, and the professional arena that we have ample opportunity to be spectators and to become loyal fans. Most Americans have their favorite sport, favorite teams, and favorite players and coaches. As a player or a spectator, it is easy to get caught up in the excitement of the offense. After all, that is where we get to run with the ball, or shoot and score, or hit and run or whatever we do to help our team accumulate points to win the game. But most of the time the coach is more interested in defense, instructing us to stay in our positions and protect our area from the opposing team to keep them from scoring. There's a reason for that. What happens if they get too far ahead of you? Speaking as a former softball player and as a parent of a basketball player, when the opposing team gets too much lead, you feel like giving up. When you know that you can't possibly overcome the deficit, you don't feel like trying anymore. You are just waiting for the closing buzzer to sound so you can get off the field or court. But as long as you can keep your defense strong and prevent the other team from running away from you <u>and</u> generate a little offense, your interest and your efforts stay peaked until the game is over.

How many of us realize that is a lot like our spiritual battle? Some of us get so caught up in the offense that we forget about our defense. If you will continue to read in our selected passage today about the pieces of spiritual armor that Paul describes, take note that all but one are defensive or protective in nature. And the very first instruction from our "coach" in these verses is to "stand firm." Standing firm in our faith is one of the strongest witnesses we can display. How many of us, however, since we've been Christians have felt at times as if we were on a spiritual "Slip 'N Slide"? We go forward one step and then slide back two. We gain a little ground in an area, then let our defenses down, and let the devil come right back in and reclaim it. If we let him gain or claim enough ground in our lifestyle, we are in danger of feeling defeated and we adopt that "why try?" attitude. And even if he doesn't totally defeat us, he can certainly score enough points to distract us from our kingdom goal, and discredit our witness with unbelievers.

Standing firm in our faith and in our lifestyle is important. Protect your goal! Remember all those defensive drills. Remember that your "Coach" is always on the sidelines calling out the plays. He wants you to experience victory! Sweet victory!

Prayer thought: Lord, today I am acknowledging You as my "Coach" in this game of life. I have been made aware today of the importance of defense. I also understand that the devil's team doesn't play fairly, which makes it even more vitally important that I listen to You and Your instructions. Help me to stand firm! Help me always to remember that with You as my Coach, I am always on the winning team!

Living Without Worry, Stress, or Anxiety…Can It Really Be Done?!

"Who of you by worrying can add a single hour to his life?" (Matthew 6:27)

"Do not be anxious about anything, but in everything, by prayer and petition, with thanksgiving, present your requests to God. And the peace of God, which transcends all understanding, will guard your hearts and your minds in Christ Jesus. (Phillipians 4:6-7)

Worry, stress, and anxiety are buzzwords of our times. And if we are honest, most of us could confess that we struggle with them at times. Why? Because life is so unpredictable. Just when we think we have one situation under control in our lives, something else will hit us from another side. Accompanying worry, stress, and anxiety are confusion, fear, doubt, and dread. And as we read today's scriptures, we can see that these states of mind are not how God wants us to live. God promises a peace that passes all understanding that will guard our hearts against these things. It's up to us to walk in it.

You're probably thinking, "That's a lot easier said than done." The way a lot of us allow ourselves to worry, you would think that worry is a pre-requisite to problem-solving. Actually, worry does bring results, not results to our problems, but often times it brings additions to the problems—additions like undue stress, headaches, ulcers, heart attacks, pre-mature and improper actions or decisions, imagined bleak outcomes, or dread. It is very hard for us to lead productive lives when we are fighting the physical, emotional, and spiritual side effects of worry.

On the other side of the coin, walking in peace in times of outside turmoil is one of the greatest forms of witness we can show to the unsaved world. Unbelievers are seeking inner peace that results in a quieting of the turmoil in their lives that can only come through a genuine relationship with God. They need to see it manifested in our lives. Believe me, Satan knows that. He also knows that by keeping the pressure turned up on us there's a better chance we will allow stress and worry to enter in and push trust and peace out. And what we feel on the inside becomes visible on the outside. The unbeliever then doesn't see anything different about how we react to things than the rest of the world reacts.

I'm not saying all this to make us feel guilty about succumbing to worry, but to make us more aware of the promises of God in this area. The Bible is full of these promises. God will help us walk "through" the valleys. He may not always totally lift us out of our circumstances, but He will definitely be there while we are going through them. Situations do not last forever. God's love does.

How do we keep from worrying and being stressed out? It's a replacement principle. Visualize this object lesson. Fill a cup or glass with a dark liquid, such as coffee or soda and set it in a sink or basin. The dark liquid represents worry. Fill a pitcher with water. The clear water represents peace. If you begin to pour the clear peace into the glass or cup containing the dark worry, it will eventually push all the worry out, and your cup will be filled with peace. But if you don't lift your arm to pour the clear peace in, the dark worry will stay in your cup. Peace is available, but we have to exercise our trust in God to fill our lives with it.

Prayer thought: Oh Lord, how often have I given in to worry, stress, and anxiety in my daily life! Jesus, You know the struggles that I am going through. Help me to remember and to act on the words of today's passage. It is very important for my own physical, emotional, and spiritual well being and it is very important for those who are examining my life for answers they are seeking. Thank You, Lord Jesus, for making available to me the peace that passes all understanding. I will begin today to trust You to replace my worry with that peace.

Following the Leader

"Enter through the narrow gate. For wide is the gate and broad is the road that leads to destruction, and many enter through it. But small is the gate and narrow the road that leads to life, and only a few find it." (Matthew 7:13-14)

Did you ever play "Follow the Leader" as a child? It was the leader's job to make the course or the path interesting. He didn't walk in a straight line across the playground. Depending on how agile he was, he would climb over, crawl under, twist, turn, and jump around things to see how many had the agility and stamina to follow his lead. If you've ever been to an aerobics or exercise class, you know that the instructor stands in front of the class and demonstrates the proper way to move and stretch. The class then follows the instructor's lead and tries to repeat the actions. And as painful or tiring as this may be for thirty minutes, we are willing to follow her lead in order to achieve certain desired results in our lives. My youngest daughter played basketball in high school. It was her responsibility to follow the instructions of her coach. He didn't actually get out on the floor with his team, but he was always there to lay out the game plan and to direct and correct them throughout the course of the grueling practices and the games. And she knew if she wanted to see a lot of playing time that she had to listen to and obey the coach.

All of the things we've been talking about are examples of short-term commitments. Most of us can handle short-term commitments because we know it will be over soon. It's the long-term commitments that give some of us problems. And by now, you probably know where I'm going with this. Following Jesus is a long-term commitment. It's a total change of our life and our life-style. As in our examples before, He will lead us through the course of our life, and it won't always be an easy path. But He wants us to stay agile and alert and keep Him in our sites. He will be our perfect example demonstrating how to live, and we are to repeat His actions. He has laid out the game plan in His book, and the Holy Spirit is always there to direct and guide us. But the game never ends. From the time we accept Him into our lives, we are to follow His lead, His example, and His instructions. And if He were the only One we had to listen to, it would be relatively simple. But there are a lot of other "leaders" out there who are trying to get us to follow them, including Satan, who tries to get us to think we should be our own leader and follow the Almighty Self and our own desires. And it all boils down to making the right choice about who we are going to follow.

Jesus tells us in our passage today that He realizes that the majority of people won' t make the commitment that it takes to follow Him. There' s a difference in being a believer and being a disciple. Sometimes we Christians are so intent on getting people saved that we try to paint them a picture of ease and comfort. We tell them about accepting Jesus as Savior, but neglect to tell them about His desire and our responsibility to make Him "Lord" of our lives as well. It is really easy to walk into church once or twice a week, say hello to God, sit through a couple of sermons, throw up a couple of prayers, walk out and say "See you next week, Lord." And to a lot of people that is their idea of Christianity. When you add the uncommitted to the multiplied millions who follow self or other leaders, no wonder Jesus says His followers are in the minority. Most people choose the path of least resistance. That is why that gate is so wide. Jesus says, "Follow me." The narrow road leads to life. Whom are you following?

Prayer thought: Lord, keep me on the narrow path. Sometimes the path You lead me on has some difficult turns. Sometimes Your examples are hard to follow. Sometimes I don' t want to follow Your instructions. But I have learned that Your way is the best way for my life. And I am in this journey with You for the long haul. And I thank You, Lord, for being the perfect Leader, the perfect Instructor, and the perfect Coach.

People Pleasing Avenue

"Be careful not to do your acts of righteousness before men, to be seen by them. If you do, you will have no reward from your Father in heaven. So when you give to the needy, do not announce it with trumpets, as the hypocrites do in the synagogues and on the streets, to be honored by men. I tell you the truth, they have received their reward in full. But when you give to the needy, do not let your left hand know what your right hand is doing, so that your giving may be in secret. Then your Father who sees what is done in secret, will reward you." (Matthew 6:1-4)

There is a big difference between religious "works" and kingdom "work." We as Christians can stay extremely busy doing work for the church, but doing it for the wrong reasons. Some of it may actually bear a little fruit for God. But we have to be very careful about "why" we serve in the church. Are we serving the God we love because we love Him? If so, God will pour out His blessings on our efforts and the fruit of our work will be plentiful. We will know that we are pleasing God. I can think of no greater reward than knowing that I am pleasing my God.

However, one of the easiest side roads to get off on in the church is People Pleasing Avenue. I know, because I've been on that road several times myself. And when I veer onto that street, almost without exception God will start nudging me in the direction of **Ephesians 6:7, *"Serve wholeheartedly, as if you were serving the Lord, not men"*** or ***Colossians 3:23, "Whatever you do, work at it with all your heart, as working for the Lord, not for men."*** He must have thought this point was worth repeating. When we become people pleasers, our motives become tainted, and we begin to do what we do for the praise or attention of man. If that is all we seek, that is all we will receive. One of the ugliest words a Christian can be called is found in verse 2. It is the word "hypocrite." Hypocrites give Christianity a bad name. Hypocrites keep the lost out of church.

Jesus begins talking in these verses and in the passages that follow about three areas of worship…giving, praying, and fasting. In this instance, when He talks about giving to the needy, He talks about giving in secret. And by that He means that you should not make a big production or announcement about the fact that you are giving or about the size of your gift. Have you ever given an anonymous gift and then never told anyone? That' s a real test of the flesh. There' s just something in us that wants some sort of recognition for the good things we do. Unselfish and discreet giving with pure motives is a form of worship. We are telling God with this type of giving, "God, as You have blessed me, let me now be a blessing to someone else. Take this gift with my love."

Prayer thought: Lord, I am asking You today to examine my motives for the things I do and then to reveal them to me. Thank You for teaching me that giving is a form of worship to You. You have given me so much. I want to give back to You out of a heart of love and not out of a need to be recognized by man. Father, I do not want to be a people-pleaser. I want to please You, Lord, because I love You.

High Profile, Low Profile, or No Profile?

"Now the body is not made up of one part but many. If the foot should say, 'Because I am not a hand, I do not belong to the body,' it would not for that reason cease to be part of the body...But in fact God has arranged the parts in the body, every one of them, just as he wanted them to be. If they were all one part, where would the body be? As it is there are many parts, but one body." (1 Cor. 12:14-15, 18-20)

High profile, low profile, or no profile...where do you fit in the area of servanthood? People in a church with pulpit ministries, pastoral titles, teaching or music ministries or who are in other highly visible leadership roles are high-profile servants. Their accomplishments or the fruits of their service are usually monitored by the numbers they reach. *How well is the pastor serving?* Well, how many are in worship service, or how many new members have we had this year? *How well is the music minister serving?* How full is the choir loft? How many people came to the Christmas and Easter programs? *How well is the youth pastor serving?* How many kids does he have on Wednesday night? *How well is a Sunday School teacher serving?* How many are active in his class? In defense of high-profile servants, because I have been one, it may not always be fair to judge their servanthood solely by the numbers. The quality of their service will be judged by our Lord according to the motivation of the heart and their genuine sacrificial attitude of serving. I can remember when I first started teaching a newly-formed Sunday School class and would study for four hours in preparation to teach. For months I would step into that class on Sunday morning, and it would just be myself and one other faithful young girl, no matter how many contacts I had made. Even though it was disappointing, I knew that I had to give her what the Lord had given me. It was a much greater sacrifice for me to prepare during that time than it was a year or so later when the room got so full we had to find a larger place to meet. And then I had people asking me for copies of my lessons when they couldn't be there, or if they lived in other cities, or attended other churches. (And those lessons are now the basis of this book.) And before I knew it, I had a room full of regular students and about twenty correspondence students. But it was no more important because there were 35 than it was when there was one. Because I knew that I didn't add the increase, God did. I supplied the service. God supplied the numbers. High-profile servants are under a lot of pressure to succeed and a great deal of temptation to personally bask in God's glory when they do. When that happens, the servant's heart is replaced by personal desires of success. That's when you see so many big-time ministries fall. So pray for the leaders in your church that their hearts will remain pure, their motives will remain sacrificial, and that God can use them to touch one or a thousand.

Low-profile servants are those people in your church who are like the Energizer bunny. They just keep going and going and going, and you never really notice them. They are behind-the-scenes servants. They are the helpers. They're the ones the church can always count on to bring food, clean up, decorate, sit in the nursery, visit shut-ins, and on and on. Most of the time, they have no desire to be "up-front," but their ministry is vitally important. If you start pulling those people out of a church, it doesn't matter how good your leadership is, the church cannot survive. In fact, the low-profile servants are the ones who most closely exemplify the heart of Christ. We, as a church, need to remember that as we encourage each other in the Lord. Don't heap all your praise and encouraging words on the people with the high-profile gifts. Remember the servants whom you don't notice quite so readily, but who are always there, always willing to do "whatever," and who are not really expecting any pats on the back. They just do what they do as unto the Lord. These people are your anchors. They keep your church stable during the storms. When the preacher leaves, or when the minister of music changes, or when your Sunday School teacher steps down, it's the anchor people that keep the ship from sinking. Don't let a week go by without acknowledging someone "behind the scenes."

If you are a no-profile person, that means that you haven't moved into an area of sacrificial service. You're a pew-sitter. And that's okay for a little while, but God won't let you do that very long before He starts putting some area or someone on your heart to serve. A lot of people, however, get really adept at turning down the volume on God's voice when He starts impressing service on their hearts. But let me just tell you from experience that until you start giving away God's love and blessings through sacrificial service, there's a limit to how much you can receive from Him. He didn't call us out of sin and into eternal life with Him simply to be Sunday morning sponges. Find your place of service. You'll never know how God can use you until you offer yourself to Him. You may be the next Billy Graham, or you may be a vital part of your church's "anchor" system.

Prayer thought: Father, show me that place where You would have me serve. If You're calling me into leadership, I know that You will equip me for it. Keep my motives pure.

Lord, if there's a low-profile place of service in my church where I can serve, reveal it to me. Show me what my role is in the body where You've placed me. Also, Lord, help me consciously to be aware of the sacrificial services of the rest of the church body. I commit, Lord, to be a source of prayer and encouragement for both the high-profile and low-profile servants in my church.

Pick that Up and Follow Me

"Then He called the crowd to him along with the disciples and said: 'If anyone would come after me, he must deny himself and take up his cross and follow me.'" (Mark 8:34)

So many people miss the boat with Christianity because they are duped into thinking that "acknowledging" Jesus Christ as Savior is all there is to it. "Yes, I believe in God." "Yes, I believe that Jesus died on the cross and rose on the third day." "Yes, I am saved."

Well, obviously, we have to acknowledge someone's presence before we can follow him. But it is not in our acknowledgment of Christ that we grow to be more like Him. It is in our following Him. We know that to be true in our human relationships. Suppose a teenage mother gives birth to a baby, but then leaves the baby to the grandparents to raise. When the child grows up, he may acknowledge his mother as his mother, but he will more closely resemble the people whom he has followed around for twenty years. Our character is shaped by relationships with people whose lives we choose to look to as examples. We don't have a lot of choice, however, in parental or family role models. And that is why we have a lot of poor character development from people following poor examples. But praise God, once we've been introduced to Jesus Christ, we have the perfect example to follow. And then we need to carefully examine the human examples in our lives against His standards of living to make sure we don't get pulled back into emulating the imperfect.

But Jesus also said in this verse that we have to deny ourselves, take up our cross and follow Him. That tells me it is not always going to be easy. When we first come to Christ and are full of eagerness and new-found strength, we're pumped and ready to carry our cross. But then the road starts going uphill, the cross starts getting heavier, and our arms and back start to get tired. That's when many want to just drop it and run back into the world, because Satan says, "It's not worth it. It's easier over here." Well, we all know that's a lie. We know that the cross of Christ is an instrument of redemption for His followers and it gets heavy sometimes, but we also know that in it lies life. But the crosses of the world are there, too. And if we lay down His cross, we will pick up another one. And those crosses are instruments of death. Maybe you' ve seen some people carrying some of them: addictions, apathy, rebellion, selfishness, cruelty, jealousy, bitterness, pride…maybe you' ve even carried them yourself. If so, then you must realize that they are much heavier than the cross of Christ. Which are you carrying now?

Prayer thought: Lord Jesus, this day I choose to follow the example You've shown me. I live in a world of multiple choices. But I know, Jesus, that You are the only answer. Help me to stay so close to You that Your character becomes my character. Lord, I've carried too many of the crosses of this world in my life. They were dead weight. From now on, Lord, let Your cross be the only cross I carry.

Atoning Blood

"God presented Him as a sacrifice of atonement, through faith in His blood." (Romans 3:25a)

God has always required blood to atone for sins, because life is contained in the blood. And He required something perfect to cover the imperfect. But the mere ritual of sprinkling blood on the atonement cover in Old Testament times, or the actual blood of Jesus that was shed on the cross, has no meaning unless we have faith in its atoning quality. We say over and over to people that Jesus died on the cross for you and for me, and in His blood lies the forgiveness of our sins, but unless we <u>believe</u> it, the blood does not cover us.

Was there enough blood shed on the cross for all of mankind? Yes. Will it be applied to every life? No. Salvation is available to "all" believers. It is available to all of us who activate our faith. It is available to all of us who realize that we are sinners and are in need of a Savior. It is available to all of us who are ready to receive the free gift and to acknowledge the sacrifice made and the atoning power of the blood. There is no fine print. There is no single, grand prizewinner. What we receive is eternal life, which means heaven. But it means more than that. It means a new life here on earth. It doesn't necessarily mean a perfect set of circumstances, but a new way of life and of dealing with our circumstances. It means a joy and a peace that you can't explain. It means that you have found a new relationship with the Creator of the universe. There is no reason for anyone to turn down this offer, but sadly enough, many do. Don't let that be you. Believe on the Lord Jesus Christ and the power of His blood and you will be saved.

Prayer thought: Jesus, thank You for Your precious blood that You poured out freely for me. Your perfect life, Your perfect blood, became the perfect cleansing agent for my filthy sins. There was nothing that I could offer Holy God to make up for the failures in my life, but I didn't have to. Instead He offered You for me. Thank You, Jesus.

But We've Always Done It That Way!

"The Pharisees and some of the teachers of the law who had come from Jerusalem gathered around Jesus and saw some of his disciples eating food with hands that were 'unclean', that is unwashed. (The Pharisees and all the Jews do not eat unless they give their hands a ceremonial washing, holding to the tradition of the elders.) (Mark 7:1-3)

How many of us have ever broken a rule? If you have ever colored outside the lines or substituted an ingredient in a recipe or arrived fifteen minutes late for a party, then in a sense, you have broken rules. There were written guidelines to follow, and you chose not to follow them. In the sixties, we called that "freedom of expression." What about tradition? It's just understood that we eat our dessert last. It's just understood that Thanksgiving dinner will be at Grandma's house and that Aunt Helen will be bringing candied yams. It's just understood that your family will be taking their vacation the first week in August. Sometimes we do things just because that's the way they've always been done. Sometimes there's merit to tradition. Sometimes there's logic. Sometimes the reasons get lost. And then there are laws. When we get into the realm of breaking laws, there is far less allowance for "freedom of expression." If you've ever felt your stomach rise to your chest when you've looked in your rear-view mirror and seen flashing red lights behind you, you know what I'm talking about.

As individuals, as citizens, as Christians we need to discern and obey the rules, traditions, and laws that matter. God is more interested in us following those rules that He writes on our heart than the traditions handed down by man. Now, we need to be careful and not return to the rebellious attitudes of the sixties and throw all restraint out of the window. We need to examine the "why" behind the act to see if a command of God is in it. A lot of the things we do in a church have very good Biblical standards behind them, and those things we should embrace and continue to affirm. For example, the observance of the Lord's Supper, the teaching of the Word, baptizing believers, gathering together to pray, equipping each other to reach the lost, coming together to worship as a corporate body of Christ are important. We just need to be careful that the "how" we do these things does not overshadow the "why" we do them.

In our scripture passage today we see the group of people that Jesus frequently used as a teaching example of "what a Christian is not." The Pharisees. Unfortunately, until Jesus came along to expose them, they were looked to as the perfect religious examples. The Pharisees were always on the lookout for ways to discredit Jesus and His followers. They had done the same thing with John the Baptist. The Pharisees knew they were in danger of losing the people to this new, radical, less-than-religious Way. Those pious, over-critical, judgmental Pharisees! We can read these scriptures and see right through to their self-centered, unbending, better-than-you, ugly hearts! What possible difference could it make in the furtherance of the kingdom of God whether or not we go through some ten-minute, showy, ceremonial hand-washing before we eat! They had taken a perfectly good principle, cleanliness, and added their own rules for <u>the</u> standard of acceptable behavior.

Now before we burn all the Pharisees at the stake, take a look inside our own churches today and I'm sure you'll find at least one Pharisee on every pew, or at least some with a few Pharisaic tendencies. You may not have to look any farther away than to the person wearing your shoes. As Baptists, Methodists, Catholics, Pentecostals, Lutherans, non-denominationals, etc., we all have our views on the "how to's." We refer to ourselves as "we" and to everybody else as "they." We analyze to death the way <u>they</u> do things instead of examining the "why" or the commands of God behind it that ultimately should bring persons into a closer personal relationship with Jesus Christ. Within our own churches we allow ourselves to get so steeped in tradition and opposed to change that we lose sight of the reason practices were initiated in the first place. And in so doing, we box ourselves in and box others out. Ceremonial hand-washing was not a major kingdom problem, yet the Pharisees had made it into one. Ask yourself that question the next time you're tempted to judge or criticize someone or something within or outside your own church. Is this a major kingdom problem, or a personal preference problem? Am I doing this because that' s the way it has always been done? Do I even know why I do it?

Prayer thought: God, help me not to get boxed in to a set of rules and regulations that become full of religion and void of relationship with You. Teach me those things that are important and free me from those things that aren' t. Help me not to become so free-spirited that I lose sight of Your direction. Lord, help me to remember the words of my pastor as he encourages us in the example of Christ to "keep the main thing the main thing."

But They Are Not Like Us!

"Then some of the believers who belonged to the party of the Pharisees stood up and said, 'The Gentiles must be circumcised and required to obey the law of Moses.' The apostles and elders met to consider this question. After much discussion, Peter got up and addressed them: 'Brothers, you know that some time ago God made a choice among you that the Gentiles might hear from my lips the message of the gospel and believe. God, who knows the heart, showed that he accepted them by giving the Holy Spirit to them, just as he did to us. He made no distinction between us and them, for he purified their hearts by faith. Now then, why do you try to test God by putting on the necks of the disciples a yoke that neither we nor our fathers have been able to bear. No! We believe it is through the grace of our Lord Jesus that we are saved, just as they are.'" (Acts 15:5-11)

The statement that jumped out at me in this passage is found in verse 8, *"God, who knows the heart..."* How many people have walked the aisle of a church or dipped in baptismal waters who were no more saved than Aunt Esther's cat? They had the concept of acts confused with the concept of salvation. And yet, church members blindly accept them based on this outward act. On the other side of the coin, how many people have truly had a life-changing experience with Christ in their homes, or outside the church somewhere, but have not yet made a public confession or been obedient to follow in baptism and are rejected as members of the family of God until they do?

In our passage today, there was a discussion going on about the requirements for salvation for the Gentiles. Peter got up and spoke after "much discussion." We don't know how much discussion or how loud it was, but we do know when Peter addressed the group that he had something important to say. And that fact is evidenced by the fact that it is recorded in Scripture. Peter let them know that it was God Himself who instructed him to take the good news to the Gentiles. It was God Himself who was preparing their hearts to receive it. He was making no distinction between "them and us."

Peter also told the Gentiles that they didn' t have to meet people' s entrance requirements, only God' s. He would change them afterward.

In the following passage (vv. 13-21), Jesus' little brother James spoke up and affirmed with scripture what Peter and Barnabus were saying. That is an important lesson for us. Whatever questions are being debated, the answers are to be found in the Word of God, not in somebody' s mind. Opinions are opinions and should be stated as such. Truth is truth and can be verified in scripture. James reminded them of the words of the Prophets concerning the Gentiles. James said in essence, "God loves them. God accepts them and so should we. God' s grace is not difficult. We should not make it difficult for anyone turning to God."

How about us? Do we make the gospel difficult for people outside our circle of acceptance? Do we try to change people before we accept them, or do we simply accept them and let God do the changing? The Bible does not teach that we can change ourselves or others. That is the job of the Holy Spirit. Neither are we to try to make people over in the image of ourselves nor our elite group. We are to lift up Jesus and let Him step in and make them (and us) over into His image. *"No! We believe that is through the grace of our Lord Jesus that we are saved, just as they are."* That' s not too difficult, is it?

Prayer thought: Jesus, I want to thank you today for the free gift of grace that allowed a sinner like me to have a personal relationship with the King of Kings. Lord, help me to remember that it is not my place to put restrictions or requirements on others to join me in your family, nor to make the gospel difficult for anyone to receive. Father, forgive me if I have been guilty of categorizing or excluding anyone from hearing about your grace.

What are the Rules?

"Therefore no one will be declared righteous in His sight by observing the law, rather, through the law we become conscious of sin. But now a righteousness from God, apart from law, has been made known, to which the Law and the Prophets testify. This righteousness from God comes through faith in Jesus Christ to all who believe. There is no difference, for all have sinned and fall short of the glory of God and are justified freely by his grace through the redemption that came by Christ Jesus. (Romans 3:20-24)

Okay, suppose I would like to be saved. Where's the catch? What do I have to do? I have to follow all these rules, don't I? I'm going to have to clean up my act first, right? Wrong. You have probably heard some of these questions from non-Christians. Perhaps you have even asked them yourself. Most people know their own weaknesses and are certain that they are not going to be able to keep all the rules. This scripture says no one will be declared righteous by observing the law. If that were the end of the story, everyone would fall and there would be no winners. Well, if no one can keep the law or the rules, why even have them? They were given to us as goals and as a way of becoming conscious of sin in our lives. The first step in the salvation process is in our acknowledgment of the fact that we are sinners. If God had not given us black-and-white instructions on right and wrong choices, we would not be aware that we were doing anything contrary to His will. We would not be aware of sin. It started in the Garden. God said, "Don't eat of this tree, or you will surely die." If God had not said anything about the tree, Adam and Eve would not have known that it was "sin" to do so. <u>God gives us rules to follow in order for us to have a better life, not in order for us to be saved.</u> Even though physical death entered into the world after Adam and Eve disobeyed God, God began right at that point a reconciliation plan to bring mankind back into the possibility of enjoying eternal fellowship with Him, apart from anything we could do. *"But now a righteousness from God, apart from law, has been made known, to which the Law and the Prophets testify."*

Let's look at some common questions about God's plan of salvation and see if we can find the answers in the verses above.

Q. How do I receive this righteousness, or right standing with God, or salvation?
A. v.22 *"...through faith in Jesus Christ."*

Q. Who gets it?
A. v. 22 *"...all who believe. There is no difference."*

Q. But I'm better than some people are. Doesn't that count for anything?
A. v. 23 *"...for all have sinned and fall short of the glory of God."*

Q. How much does it cost?
A. v.24 *"...are justified freely by His grace through the redemption that came by Jesus Christ."*

In verse 24 we see that salvation if free, but that it was not cheap. The price was paid at the cross. Our faith releases God's grace to justify our sins. That means to look at them "just as if" we had never committed them. He did this by the redemptive sacrifice of Jesus Christ at Calvary. Our part is faith. God took care of everything else.

Prayer thought: Father God, thank You for showing me that I am a sinner by revealing the "rules" to me. Without them I would never have been aware of the distinction between Holy God and sinful man. But thank You, Lord, that You made provision for me to escape eternal death by sending Jesus to the cross in my place as justification for my sins.

I'm Not Your Slave

"For we know that our old self was crucified with him, so that the body of sin might be done away with, that we should no longer be slaves to sin—because anyone who has died has been freed from sin." (Romans 6:6-7)

What does the term "slavery" mean to you? We think of it in terms of the buying and selling of persons as property for the purpose of servitude. That doesn't happen any longer in the United States, and what we know of it we read as a very dark part of American history. But the concept of slavery can be likened to other bondages in our lives. How many of you ladies have ever said or at least thought, "All I am is just a slave in this house!"? We can be slaves to our jobs. There may be some who do not like the work they do or the hours they put in or the conditions they work under, but they feel as if they are trapped or unable to leave because of their "slavery" to the income it brings. Some people become slaves to addictions. Slavery is anything in our lives that causes us to "have" to do things we may not really want to do.

What is freedom then? Freedom is being released from restraints on your life. Freedom is being able to choose. Freedom is being able to do what you want to do. Sometimes people abuse their freedom. Along with the freedom to choose comes responsibility for those choices. And if people aren't careful, too much freedom can lead them right back into slavery. The sixties proved that. Free love, free sex, freedom from conforming to the rules of the establishment. All of that led to a total breakdown of morality and lifestyles that led those young people into self-imposed slavery. We soon learned that type of freedom didn't really make our lives better, it brought destruction. I said earlier that freedom is being able to do what you <u>want</u> to do. And that's where God wants to get involved in the freedom He has given us. God wants to change our "want to's." When God breaks the yokes of the bondage of sin off of us, He wants to free us to make right choices: choices that will benefit us and glorify Him. Real freedom involves the giving of ourselves willingly to God, not because we have to…because we <u>want</u> to!

Prayer thought: Lord, thank You for freeing me from the bondage of sin. Help me, God, to take responsibility for my freedom by making choices that glorify You and benefit me. Change <u>my</u> desires, O Lord, to Your desires for me so that I might enjoy and not take for granted the freedom that was purchased for me on Calvary.

Do I Really Want to Be God's Slave?

"When you were slaves to sin, you were free from the control of righteousness. What benefit did you reap at that time from the things you are now ashamed of? Those things result in death! But now that you have been become slaves to God, the benefit you reap leads to holiness, and the result is eternal life. For the wages of sin is death, but the gift of God is eternal life in Christ Jesus our Lord." (Romans 6:20-23)

Some of you may be thinking, "I don't really know for sure that I want to be a slave to righteousness." Paul says, in effect, "Let's compare the bottom line. Look back at your life and compare your life before and after Christ." For those of you who experienced salvation as a child, and have never become involved in any type of consistent sinful lifestyle, think of someone close to you who has. Paul says, *"What benefit did you reap at that time from the things you are now ashamed of?"* Things you used to love to do, that were a big part of your life, are now things that you are ashamed of and wouldn't think of doing. And whether you want to admit it or not, you were slaves to those sins. And without Christ, those things ultimately result in death. What are the benefits from salvation or regeneration? There's a new you. Your sinful lifestyle begins to change directions. Your life starts to count for something eternal. Yes, you're still a slave, but what a wonderful new Master you have! The benefits of salvation will start to show in your life. You will start making a much greater percentage of right decisions. You will be on the road of obedience, which leads to holiness, which leads to a more fruitful life with great blessings added. And, oh yes, there's another good bottom line comparison on the balance sheet of life…verse 23. *"For the wages of sin is death, but the gift of God is eternal life in Christ Jesus our Lord."* Now really, is there any comparison? We will be slaves to something in our lives. Let it be Jesus. You will find no greater Master. There is nothing this world has to offer that can satisfy like He can.

Prayer thought: Lord, I understand now that to be Your slave is the best thing for my life. I remember the days of my slavery to sin and the fleeting so-called "pleasures" of the world. All of those things were meant to destroy me. None of them compares with the promise of eternal life that is mine since I surrendered my life to You. Thank You for bringing me out of the darkness and into the Light.

Are You Obeying Your Master?

"For sin shall not be your master, because you are not under law, but under grace. What then? Shall we sin because we are not under law but under grace? By no means! Don't you know that when you offer yourselves to someone to obey him as slaves, you are slaves to the one whom you obey—whether you are slaves to sin, which leads to death, or to obedience, which leads to righteousness? But thanks be to God that, though you used to be slaves to sin, you wholeheartedly obeyed the form of teaching to which you were entrusted. You have been set free from sin and have become slaves to righteousness. I put this in human terms because you are weak in your natural selves. Just as you used to offer the parts of your body in slavery to impurity and to ever-increasing wickedness, so now offer them in slavery to righteousness leading to holiness." (Romans 6:14-19)

"Sin shall not be your master, because you are not under the law, but under grace." This confused the Romans. Has it ever confused us? "Well, if we're not under the law and we are under grace, it really doesn't matter if we sin or how much we sin, right?" How did Paul answer that one? **"By no means!"** You're missing the point here, folks! **"Don't you know that when you offer yourselves to someone to obey him as slaves, you are slaves to the one you obey—whether you are slaves to sin, which leads to death, or to obedience, which leads to righteousness."** Grace is not a license to sin, but rather a ticket to freedom from sin, which starts on the road of obedience. Here again we get back to the question, "Who is in control of your life…who's on the throne? Is it Christ or Self?" We will be slaves to that person. And from all the testimonies I've ever heard, I've never heard one person who ever regretted turning over the throne to Jesus. He can make much more out of our lives than we ever could even imagine. In fact, most of us when serving Self can make some pretty big messes.

I think a key phrase in today's scripture passage is found in verse 17…*"you wholeheartedly obeyed the form of teaching to which you*

were entrusted. " If you want to see a dramatic change in your life, if you want to see sinful behavior start to disappear from your lifestyle, if you want to start consistently making right choices in your life…then start disciplining yourself to "wholeheartedly obey the form of teaching to which you have been entrusted." Aim for righteousness or holiness. You just might be surprised how much better you become at hitting it. How many of us get up from our Bible study, or leave a sermon, and take those teachings and "wholeheartedly" apply them to our lives? We may walk out and say, "That was a good scripture, or lesson, or a good sermon," but until we actively put it into practice in our lives, it hasn' t really set us free from anything. When we wholeheartedly start obeying God' s words to us, we will start seeing those chains break off our lives. We then make the turn to becoming slaves to righteousness, not because we have to, but because we have chosen to.

Prayer thought: Dear God, thank You for Your grace in my life. Help me, though, never to cheapen it by rationalizing willful sin choices in my life. Father, if I can just learn what it means to wholeheartedly obey Your Word, I will begin to experience the true freedom that is mine in Christ Jesus. This is the desire of my heart, O God.

The Sign of Authority

"Pilate had a notice prepared and fastened to the cross. It read: JESUS OF NAZARETH, THE KING OF THE JEWS. Many of the Jews read this sign, for the place where Jesus was crucified was near the city, and the sign was written in Aramaic, Latin and Greek. The chief priests of the Jews protested to Pilate, 'Do not write The King of the Jews, but that this man claimed to be king of the Jews.' Pilate answered, 'What I have written, I have written.'" (John 19:19-22)

You can' t hide the truth. It doesn' t matter whether the authority of Jesus is widely accepted or not. It is fact. Pilate had just been a party to the crucifixion of a man in whom he had found no fault. He had tried to release Him. He tried to reason with the Jews. He tried to bargain with them about using the Passover pardon of a prisoner. He tried to get Jesus to rescind His statements or say something that would satisfy the Jews to keep the crucifixion from happening. He asked the King of Kings, *"Don' t you realize I have the authority to have you killed or to set you free?" Jesus said, "You don' t have any authority over me except what is given to you from above."* The Jews were intent on destroying this man and the uproar that He was causing by His claims to be the Son of God, sent from the Father, the only way to get to God. Those statements backed up by the miracles, the teachings and the perfect example of His sinless life were more than they could combat with verbal counter-attacks. His followers would have to see Him destroyed in order to discredit Him and His claim to divine authority. Jewish leaders certainly didn' t want that sign over His head in case someone mistook it for the truth. The Father saw to it that Pilate exercised his authority in the matter. *"What I have written, is written."* It was the last thing Pilate could do for Him.

They couldn' t hide the truth then, and we won' t hide the truth when He returns. Get ready. When the trumpet sounds, all questions of Christ' s authority will be answered. *"Look, He is coming with the clouds, and every eye will see Him, even those who pierced Him."*

(Rev. 1:7) The return of the King will not be in the form of the newborn in the lowly feeding trough of Bethlehem. It will not be the ripped, torn, and battered body of the Sacrificial Lamb. It will be the triumphant and majestic Lord of Lords and King of Kings in all of His glory and heavenly splendor. It will be a time when <u>all</u> will acknowledge His authority. This mighty King is Jesus. And He is the same Jesus who is alive and well in the hearts and lives of believers today. At the time we accept Him as Savior we should also accept Him as Lord and give Him that place of kingship in our lives. We shouldn't wait until the trumpet sounds to submit to His authority. We should be submitting to His Holy Spirit every day of our lives. But in order to do that we have to first take ourselves off the throne of our lives and give Jesus His proper place. My experience in submission to His authority is that I have never been sorry or disappointed in the outcome of my obedience to His decisions. I can't say the same for the times when I haven't.

The bottom line is that Jesus <u>is</u> the King. We can submit to Him now, or submit to Him later. He is a loving ruler who only wants the best for His followers. You couldn't ask for a better King.

Prayer thought: Jesus, I acknowledge that You are the King of all kings. Help me, Lord, to submit daily to Your authority in my life.

Give God the Reins

"Therefore do not let sin reign in your mortal body so that you obey its evil desires. Do not offer the parts of your body to sin, as instruments of wickedness, but rather offer yourselves to God." (Romans 6:12-13)

When we read this passage of scripture, we automatically think of sexual sins, and indeed, I believe Paul was addressing this problem with the Romans. But how many of you know that there are other parts of your body that can be used as "instruments of wickedness"? I know a lot of people…good, faithful church people…who wouldn' t think of committing sexual sins, but who may use other parts of their bodies in ways they shouldn' t. I'm thinking primarily about our tongue, or the words we speak. I say "we" because I know that there have been words come out of my mouth that were destructive instruments, and I'm very sorry for them. And we could all shrug our shoulders and say, "Oh, well, everybody does that once in a while." And even though that is true, we shouldn' t treat it as acceptable. Paul says we (Christians) are not to let sin <u>reign</u> in our mortal bodies. There is only room for one throne in our heart with only one occupant. And it is either Christ or self. Self tends to choose behavior patterns that satisfy the flesh. And it doesn' t take long for our bodies to become accustomed to that, thus the evil desires Paul is talking about here. But as Christians we have been given the "freedom" to choose not to do those things. And if we don' t exercise our freedom but allow our flesh to have control, we are allowing sin a foothold into our lifestyle. And if sin gets a foothold, it doesn' t take long for it to gain a stronghold. "Well, how can I keep that from happening? I'm not perfect. I know I am going to make wrong choices once in a while." The answer to that question is to begin to exercise your freedom to make <u>more</u> right (righteous) choices than wrong. Offer yourself to God. The longer you walk with Him and listen to Him, the more right choices you will make with less and less effort on your part. Replace sinful activity with activity that is not sinful. Use the parts of your body as "instruments of righteousness."

You do have a choice and you do have the freedom to make the right one. Turn loose of the reins and let God reign.

Prayer thought: Father, I give You control of my life. I've tried it my way, Lord, and found myself wandering off the course You set for me. Help me to walk in the freedom of my salvation by not allowing sin to reign in my mortal body. Holy Spirit, You will give me clear instruction for making right choices in my life. I offer my whole self to You. Use me as an instrument of righteousness.

Acknowledge Your Power Source

"Therefore I glory in Christ Jesus in my service to God. I will not venture to speak of anything except what Christ has accomplished through me in leading the Gentiles to obey God by what I have said and done." (Romans 15:17-18)

How many times have you heard someone say, "If God calls you to do something, He will give you the power to accomplish it."? I'm sure I've even given that assurance myself to someone questioning his ability to answer a call on his life. And I offer that with confidence because I've seen it borne out in so many lives.

However, I've also seen people who are seeing the power of God working in their lives and ministries begin to take or receive personal credit for God's results. We are God's servants. He allows us to <u>participate</u> in His work. As we begin to see people getting saved and turning their lives over to the Lord by means of any measure of our involvement, we need to maintain Paul's attitude in today's verses. I don't know how many people I've been with as they gave their lives to the Lord, but it has been quite a few. They are not my trophies, but God's. When my daughter was younger, I had to correct her after I heard her giving her testimony to someone. She was telling them how Billy Graham saved her. Even though she knew better, it was just a child's inability to express herself correctly. And even though Billy Graham has been instrumental in thousands of salvations, he, more than anyone, knows that people don't save other people. The Holy Spirit opens our eyes to the saving grace of Christ and Him crucified. Even though I quote Phillipians 4:13 as often as anybody, *"I can do all things through Christ who strengthens me,"* I also know the reality of John 15:5 as Jesus said, *"...apart from me you can do nothing."*

Paul goes on here to talk about the power that accompanies our call. God will show Himself in whatever way it takes to draw people to Him. And more often than in any other way, we are His showpieces. So if God lays on your heart to witness to or to pray for somebody,

He will give you the power to do it. Personally, I am not of the opinion that signs and miracles are a thing of the past. I believe that He is the same yesterday, today, and forever. I believe that if God wants to move through somebody in a miraculous way that He will do just that. We need to be careful, however, just as in our Billy Graham example, that we don' t begin to put our faith in people for something that God is doing. The Lord used Paul to heal the sick, cast out demons, and perform various other miracles. And I'm sure the public began looking to him for those miracles. Paul was careful to point to Jesus as the source of all miraculous things. Paul was simply a vessel available to be used. We must also realize that divine healing or sudden deliverance is not the only clear sign that God is at work. Nothing is more miraculous than the changed life of a sinner saved by grace.

Prayer thought: Father, thank You for the opportunity of participating in Your work. Lord, help me always to remember that I am powerless to bring about Godly results without the power of the Holy Spirit. Let every accomplishment of the particular assignments You give me bring glory to You and You alone.

Who's the Boss?

"Slaves, obey your earthly masters in everything; and do it, not only when their eye is on you and to win their favor, but with sincerity of heart and reverence for the Lord. Whatever you do, work at it with all your heart, as working for the Lord, not for men, since you know that you will receive an inheritance from the Lord as a reward. It is the Lord Christ you are serving. Anyone who does wrong will be repaid for his wrong, and there is no favoritism. Masters, provide your slaves with what is right and fair, because you know that you also have a Master in heaven." (Colossians 3:22-4:1)

Finding a job that you enjoy and people that you like to work for is a real blessing. After all, we spend a lot of time at our workplaces. This verse talks about slaves, because of the time period in which it was written, but it can be equated with paid workers today. How many of us work differently when the boss is in the room than when we are alone? We shouldn't. If we know what is expected of us on our jobs, we should be working the same way to accomplish it, whether or not we are being supervised. After all, Paul says, whatever we do, we should be working at with our whole heart, and that includes our hands, our minds, and our attitudes. I don't know about you, but I think my attitude about work would always be nearer to being right if I would continually remind myself that Jesus Christ is my boss.

How many of us have prayed for "favor" with our bosses or those in authority over us? That's a perfectly acceptable prayer for the child of God. But verse 25 in our focal passage today is a stark reminder of a spiritual truth or principle that applies to both believers and nonbelievers in the workplace. *"Anyone who does wrong will be repaid for his wrong, and there is no favoritism."* In fact, as a believer, when I read this, it reminds me of the higher expectations that God places on me as His representative in the world's arena. Because we spend so much time at our places of employment, usually interacting with many people, both saved and unsaved, Satan will use whatever means he can to tempt us to sin. Why? He wants to destroy our witness and to hurt us. It is his purpose (read John 10:10). What are some of the vehicles that Satan uses in the workplace? Here are a few that I have seen and experienced: stress, fatigue, greed, jealousy, gossip, disparity, disunity, self-pity, contagious negative attitudes, hurt feelings, feeling unappreciated, etc. Maybe you saw your problem area in that list, or maybe you could add a half-dozen more. The bottom line is that if we give in to any of these ploys of the enemy that result in our "wrong-doing," we shouldn' t think that we can pray ourselves out of the consequences. (v. 25) It is extremely important that we remember who is our boss. (v.23)

And then there is a word to all of you who may be owners of a business, or managers, or supervisors. Treat those working under you with respect. Treat them fairly. Treat them the way you would want to be treated. And always remember that just because you have some authority here, there is still someone higher to whom you must answer.

Prayer thought: Father, help me to be what You have called me to be at my workplace, a light, a beacon of hope, a representative of You, Lord. Help me to be on guard when I'm attacked with stress or fatigue, or any of the other things on our list. Help me to realize that not only will I bear the consequences of my wrong choices, but also the eternal soul of someone watching me may hang in the balance. Jesus, I have told You many times at the altar and in song that "I surrender all." That should mean that You are the ultimate authority in my life. Help me always to remember "who' s the boss."

Do I Have To?

"Do not think that I have come to abolish the Law or the Prophets; I have not come to abolish them but to fulfill them. I tell you the truth, until heaven and earth disappear, not the smallest letter, the least stroke of a pen, will by any means disappear from the Law until everything is accomplished. Anyone who breaks one of the least of these commandments and teaches others to do the same will be called least in the kingdom of heaven, but whoever practices and teaches these commands will be called great in the kingdom of heaven. For I tell you that unless your righteousness surpasses that of the Pharisees and the teachers of the law, you will certainly not enter the kingdom of heaven." (Matthew 5:17-20)

Jesus was attacked for his apparent "disobedience" to the Law of Moses. We know, of course, that Jesus never disobeyed the Laws of God because to do so would have been sin against God, and Jesus never sinned. At times, however, He did deviate from the added religious laws of man that confused people. Jesus said, **"I did not come to abolish the Law but to fulfill it."** He was talking about the perfect laws of God. Even though we live under the new covenant and have experienced the total forgiveness offered to us by His blood as the perfect and final sacrifice, in no way does that give us the freedom to continue to live in sin. The Ten Commandments or the Laws of God given to Moses are still the standards for us to live by. Jesus' life became the perfect example of the fulfilled Law. He took us to a new degree of obedience. He released us from the letter of the Law, which bound us up in "have to' s," and brought us into obedience based on the Spirit of the Law, which changes our actions and reactions based on our "want to' s." Do we fail? Yes. But there is now provision for our failures. But Jesus is very clear about "purposeful" sin and the message we send to others about it. **"Anyone who breaks one of the least of these commandments and <u>teaches</u> others to do the same will be called least in the kingdom of heaven."** Jesus is the fulfillment of the Law. He conquered sin and death in His own life, and He conquers it in mine daily, through my obedience to Him. And don' t think for a moment that other people do not notice your obedience or disobedience to the Laws of God. They do.

Jesus made a harsh statement in verse 20 about the Pharisees. I'm sure that this really confused the people because they considered the Pharisees and the teachers of the law to be the example of righteousness. Jesus, however, saw through their acts of righteousness as just that…acts. Their hearts were not changed. Their motivation was not to exalt God, but to exalt themselves. News flash! Jesus can see through us, too! What kind of righteousness does God demand from us then? Righteousness that is driven from our desire to please the God who saved us. Righteousness that is based on love and obedience and not fear of failure. Righteousness that manifests itself in our lives as salt and light in a corrupt and dark world. Righteousness that produces fruit for the kingdom of God. Righteousness that is consistent and steadfast. One of the greatest compliments anyone can give you is to tell the world that you are "real" or "genuine" when speaking of your walk with God. The world can spot a phony. Don' t be a Pharisee.

Prayer thought: Thank You, Jesus, for Your perfect example of obedience. Lord, help me to remember that my decision to live for You did not come with a list of things I "have to do," but with a new heart that changed the things I "want to do." Help me to make Your standards my standards for daily living.

Who's In Charge Here?

"Obey your leaders and submit to their authority. They keep watch over you as men who must give an account. Obey them so that their work will be a joy, not a burden, for that would be of no advantage to you." (Hebrews 13:17)

We're going to look at the word "authority" today. There are a lot of different kinds and levels of authority governing our lives. For example, authorities in our homes might be parents, grandparents, or maybe older siblings at times. How about the authorities in our schools? Teachers, administrators, student government, club leaders, bus drivers, hall monitors. At work? Owners, supervisors, managers, board of directors. The military has its authority set up by rank. The election process determines our government's chain of command. What about the authority in our churches? Pastors, deacons, elders, staff members, teachers, and ushers.

It would seem that in all areas of our lives there is some sort of structured authority in place. Sometimes we ourselves are placed in positions of authority. Some people thrive on authority and power and may misuse it. Others may not like the responsibilities of authority or decision making and do a poor job in those roles. But God has established structure in this world with certain chains of command to be followed in order to avoid chaos. Sometimes we disregard God's structure in our relationships, and we experience that chaos, sometimes subdued and sometimes overt. As Christians, we need to understand, respect, and submit to the authorities in our lives (so long as it doesn't contradict the Word of God). Rebelling against those who have authority over us can be a billboard sign to the world and a warning sign to us that we have not submitted to the authority of Jesus Christ over our lives. The ultimate authority, the supreme decision-maker, the final power, belongs to the King of creation, the King of Kings, Jesus Christ. *"All authority in heaven and on earth has been given to me." (Matthew 28:18)* Once we have surrendered our lives to Christ and His authority over us, learning to submit to the human authorities in our lives becomes much easier.

Prayer thought: Father, work in me an attitude of submission to the authorities in my life. First of all to You, Lord Jesus, because I want You to be the ultimate authority in my life, as I follow Your direction in all my daily decisions. But also, Lord, to those human authorities that are in place in my life. Let my submission to them be a direct reflection of my total submission to You.

No Middle Ground

"He will punish those who do not know God and do not obey the gospel of our Lord Jesus. They will be punished with everlasting destruction and shut out from the presence of the Lord and from the majesty of His power on the day He comes to be glorified in His holy people and to be marveled at among all those who have believed. This includes you, because you believed our testimony to you." (2 Thessalonians 1:8-10)

We've talked about God's love and the relief that He offers to believers. And for those of us who have relationship with Him, we can most likely testify to that love and comfort. But just as surely as the love of God is a truth for believers, the judgment of God talked about in these verses is a truth for non-believers. God's character is perfect. A lot of people prefer to focus on the love of God, but He is also a just God, a righteous God, and a holy God with no tolerance for sin. Hell is real and hell is eternal. One of the things that makes hell "hell" is found in verse 9, *"...they will be shut out from the presence of the Lord and from the majesty of His power..."* I don't recall how many times I've heard people rationalize mixing their love of the world's pleasures with a nominal acknowledgment of the existence of God or even an obligatory observance of some form of organized religion with statements like, "The God I know would not send people to hell." Obviously, they have not read the warning verses.

But just as surely as hell is real, the same is true for heaven. And it is not God's desire to send people to hell. On the contrary, it grieves Him that we <u>choose</u> this destiny. **"He is patient with you, not wanting anyone to perish, but everyone to come to repentance." (2 Peter 3:9)** The loving, merciful side of God created a plan of redemption that allows us to apply the blood of His Son to our sins to erase them from His sight. This perfect plan is the only way that you and I could ever attain right standing with Holy God and thus escape the punishment for our sins that is described in our focal verses. But we have to accept that as truth, acknowledge and repent of our sins, and accept His Son as our Savior. Otherwise, the first part of these verses will become reality in the lives of those who *"do not know God and do not obey the gospel of our Lord Jesus."* There is no middle ground. You cannot perch on top of the fence forever. Fence-straddlers will be counted among those who do not know God and do not obey the gospel of our Lord Jesus. Examine your heart. Where are you standing? There is still time to be counted with His holy people who will be marveled at as those who have believed. The last verse is an acknowledgment from Paul to the church at Thessalonica that they were included. Are you? If not, would you like to be?

When prayed from the heart, the following prayer will bring you into a relationship with God that will change your life forever, even into eternity.

Dear Jesus, I know that I am a sinner. I realize that those sins, if not forgiven, will bring about my eternal separation from You. And so, this day, I repent of my sins and ask for Your shed blood to cover me for eternity. I know that You died on the cross and rose again for that very reason. Holy Spirit, come into my life and change me. I surrender my life to You. Today I stand included as a believer, a child of God, a Christian. Thank You, Jesus.

Is That a Whip in My Hand?

"Then Pilate took Jesus and had him flogged. The soldiers twisted together a crown of thorns and put it on his head. They clothed him in a purple robe and went up to him again and again, saying, 'Hail, king of the Jews!' And they struck him in the face." (John 19:1-3)

Most of us recognize this scene as part of the agonizing reality of the arrest and subsequent crucifixion of Jesus. We have heard or read about the cruelty of flogging, the severe beating of exposed flesh with a long whip. The Romans intensified this torture by adding pieces of bone or metal to the leather thongs. Flogging preceded crucifixion with the intent of speeding up the death. Some did not survive this stage. Added to Jesus' physical torture was the humiliation by the soldiers and the crowd. The crown of thorns served a sadistic double purpose to his scourgers. The thorns dug deeply into his head as an added physical torture, and the twisted shape of a "crown" was meant to make fun or light of His "kingship," as was the purple robe. I am sure the laughter, the jeers, and the humiliating remarks cut just as deeply into the human side of Jesus as did the whips. But the divine side of Jesus was evidenced in His words on the cross for the very ones who had done all these evil things to Him. *"Father, forgive them, for they know not what they do."*

Have there ever been times in our lives when we have mocked Jesus? "I would <u>never</u> mock Jesus," you might say. Have we ever laughed or made fun of someone's mistakes or shortcomings? Surely Jesus has taught us better than that. Have we ever told a lie to make our life easier or to keep from being obedient to God? Have we ever purposely hung on to a particular sin in our life, relying on God's grace and the shed blood to cover it? Do we disregard His principles when they are inconvenient in our lives? What about the times when we have been around people who take the Lord's name in vain? Does it hurt us to the point of saying something, or do we just ignore it and let the pain it causes Him go unanswered? We say we love Him, yet we fail to defend His honor. Or, heaven forbid, maybe there have been times when we have spoken His name in an irreverent way.

How He must wince as that verbal whip tears across His back! We need to begin to realize that when we ignore His teaching, we ignore Him and mock His authority in our lives. In fact, any time we publicly and adamantly profess to bear the name of Christian, and then compromise His values and standards, we degrade Him and flog Him all over again.

Prayer thought: Jesus, those men who scourged You in Jerusalem did not have a relationship with You. They did not know You. I do. I see now that when I fail to recognize Your authority in my life and disregard the sacrifice You made for me by compromising my lifestyle, that I must leave even deeper and more painful cuts. Jesus, it is not my desire to cause You pain. Oh Lord, please forgive me for the times I've held that whip in my hand!

Don' t Let the Devil Sneak Up on You!

"The thief comes only to steal, kill and destroy. I have come that they may have life, and have it to the full." (John 10:10)

I am relatively certain that most of us can stop and think about something that Satan has stolen or destroyed in our lives. That' s his sole purpose and he does it very well. Sometimes he is blatant, but most of the time he is subtle. For example, suppose you walked out of your house one day and your car was missing. You would immediately know that someone had stolen it, and you would begin to react. But suppose someone came into your home during the Christmas season and took a single ornament off your tree. You probably wouldn' t even notice it until you began taking your tree down and maybe not even then. The next year you might start wondering, "What happened to that angel ornament?" You might just be confused and still not even realize that it had been taken from you. But if it occurred systematically over a period of years, there would come a time when you would realize your tree was beginning to look bare. That' s the way it is with Satan and the things he steals from us. Sometimes we realize that he is openly trying to destroy something like our marriage or a family member, and we react immediately in standing against him in prayer and the authority we have in Jesus. But sometimes he can sneak in and start stealing our joy, our peace of mind, our spiritual desires a little at a time, and it may be a long period of time before we realize that those things are missing.

How can we protect ourselves against this thief? Jesus wants to be our protector. But we have to stay close to Him in order for Him to protect us from the thief. He wants to be the giver of the good life that can only be found in Him. When we start wandering off and leaving the door of our heart unlocked, we leave ourselves open to theft. Examine your life on a regular basis. If there are circumstances in your life that are unpleasant and are making you unpleasant, or depressed, or rebellious, stop and do a quick spiritual inventory. "Okay, before this circumstance entered my life, I had joy in the Lord and peace that passed understanding, and a lot more patience! Where are they? Devil, you are NOT going to steal them from me! You are NOT going to use this circumstance to steal from me what my Lord has given me!" But if you are not aware of what is happening, if you fail to keep track of what is yours in Christ, it may turn out like our Christmas ornament story. Long after the circumstance is over, you may not even realize that you had something stolen from you. And then before you know it, another circumstance will come along and take something else. Don' t let that happen. Trials and problems are going to come along in our lives, but Jesus said, "Don' t worry, I have overcome the world!" (John 16:33) He is our Protector against the destroyer. Keep such a close watch on your "stuff" that you immediately know when Satan is tugging on it. Don' t let the devil sneak up on you!

Prayer thought: Lord, help me always to examine my life right in the middle of my circumstances to make sure that Satan is not trying to steal what is mine. Don' t let me wait until the circumstance is over and then look back and wonder what happened.

Caught in a Trap

"Brothers, if someone is caught in a sin, you who are spiritual should restore him gently. But watch yourself, or you also may be tempted." (Galatians 6:1)

How many of you would agree that it is a lot easier for us to act kindly and lovingly toward someone who is facing hardship or sickness than it is for us to show loving concern for someone caught in sin? What kind of "caught" is Paul talking about in this verse? Does he mean "caught in a sin" as being "discovered or found out"? Or, does he mean, "caught in a sin" as one being "trapped or ensnared"? Either way, what is the Christ-like response? Paul says that you who are spiritual should ***"restore him gently."***

Let's look at the first idea of the term "caught" as it relates to our response. For the most part when someone is caught in a sin, or "discovered or found out", our first human inclination is to talk <u>about</u> them instead of talking <u>to</u> them. "Did you hear what so and so did? I just couldn't believe it. And they call themselves a Christian!" In the second case, when someone is caught or "trapped or ensnared" in a sin, our human inclination is to say, "It's none of my business. God will deal with them." It's much easier for us to turn our heads and allow them to remain "caught" than it is for us to confront them and try to get them out. Why? Because our actions may not be welcome, or our motives may be questioned. I think it is much like trying to help an animal out of a trap. It may try to bite and scratch while you're trying to free it because it doesn't understand that you are trying to help it. And you may think that it is not worth getting hurt over. After all, it was their own carelessness or blindness to the consequences of sin that entrapped them in the first place. But what happens to the animal if it remains in the trap? It will die. What happens to your friend if he or she remains in a sin trap? Are you willing to risk getting hurt or being made to feel uncomfortable to approach him or her and to be obedient to this scripture?

Paul also talks here about being careful. Yes, we should be careful about restoring those who are caught in sin. We should be careful that we are not tempted. Just as there are two connotations to the word "caught" in our scripture today, there may be two areas of danger involved in the word "tempted." We may be tempted to fall into the same sin trap as the person we are trying to free. That is a very real danger. Make sure you are prayed up and fully aware of how the trap is "baited." The ensnared victim may be more actively seeking someone to join him in the trap than to help free him. And he may drag you right in with him. Or, we may be tempted to fall into the sin of judgment. We must be very careful not to attack the victim while we are attacking the trap. We should not let our spiritual zeal for righteousness become a self-righteous attack on the sinner. If we do that, it's more likely that the person will be turned off by our "offer" of help than be turned on to the Truth that will set him free. Be careful. Restore him gently.

Prayer thought: Lord, I know people who are caught in Satan's trap. Help me not to overlook them. Help me to understand, Lord, that You want to set them free, and it might be a word or an act on my part that You use to unlock the chains. Jesus, I pray that I will not be caught in the sin of self-righteousness. Show me how to restore them gently and be mindful of the dangers of the trap.

Don't Major on Minor Issues

"Therefore let us stop passing judgment on one another. Instead, make up your mind not to put any stumbling block or obstacle in your brother's way." (Romans 14:13) "For the kingdom of God is not a matter of eating and drinking but of righteousness, peace, and joy in the Holy Spirit, because anyone who serves Christ in this way is pleasing to God and approved by men." (Romans 14:17-18)

Before coming to these verses in chapter 14 of Romans, Paul has been addressing the body of Christians at Rome concerning the acceptance or non-acceptance of certain behaviors, specifically eating and drinking certain foods and the observance of certain behaviors on certain days. Paul realized that to some of these people these practices were important, so instead of starting a major conflict over issues of minor importance, Paul instructs them not to judge or put down other people's convictions.

When we've got a church full of people all at different stages of spiritual growth, nothing is more confusing than to see people engaged in major conflicts over minor issues. Obviously, we are not talking about conflicts over biblical absolutes. It is our responsibility as Christians to correct fellow believers who are involved in or who are promoting biblically identifiable sin. But, there are certain other things that God has to deal with us individually about. For example, some church bodies have spent an incredible amount of God's time arguing over building projects, or which translation of the Bible the pastor should be using, or whether to sing hymns or choruses in worship service. Divisiveness over minor issues can majorly impact the effectiveness of a church. It is the responsibility of the leadership of the church to keep the body focused on Jesus and those areas of ministry that are kingdom-building and not kingdom-crippling.

The last two verses above puts it all into perspective. If we would stop majoring on the minors and start focusing on these three areas of our own lives…righteousness, peace, and joy in the Holy Spirit…the kingdom of God would grow by leaps and bounds, and we would see

God smiling in our lives and on our churches. We have to first realize that we are righteous, but not because of anything we've done or any rules we've kept. We are righteous only because of the blood of the Lamb. And because the blood covered my sins and I've been forgiven, that lost person down the street or that Christian on the next pew has just as much grace and forgiveness available to him as I do. Once we realize who we are in Christ, a sinner saved by grace, made clean and acceptable in the presence of Almighty God only because of Jesus, then we are able to move into that place of peace. And with that peace comes the unspeakable joy of knowing that the person of the Holy Spirit lives inside of us. If we, as Christians, can get hold of that in our everyday lives, small things will remain small, and the big thing (sharing Christ) will get bigger and evangelism will happen.

Prayer thought: Lord, I offer You this prayer of Paul's as my prayer this day. **(Romans *15:5-7*)** *"May the God who gives endurance and encouragement give* (me, my church) *a spirit of unity among* (ourselves) *as* (we) *follow Christ Jesus, so that with one heart and mouth* (we) *may glorify the God and Father of our Lord Jesus Christ.* (Help us to) *accept one another, then, just as Christ accepted* (us), *in order to bring praise to God."*

Under the Influence or Under His Influence?

"Wine is a mocker and beer a brawler; whoever is led astray by them is not wise." (Proverbs 20:1)

If I could personally interview each of my readers, I would probably be hard pressed to find someone whose life has not been touched in some way by drug or alcohol use. It may be your own personal testimony about your own struggles with their use. It may be a story about living with someone who was/is a user. It may be the painful memory of someone you loved who was killed by a drunk driver. Maybe it's a story of depression or stress that caused you or someone you loved to turn to alcohol or drugs to deaden the pain. Or perhaps it's a story of one or two isolated times in your life when you gave in to peer pressure. Some may even have "funny" stories of yourself or people you know and the uninhibited behavior displayed while under the influence. And by uninhibited behavior, I mean things that a person would never do if he were in control of his own mind. God has much to say in His word concerning the use of alcohol, and even though there is nothing specifically said about the hard drugs we have since introduced into our world, we can be sure that the same wisdom applies to those substances that have the same or even stronger mind-altering effects on us.

Because God gave man freedom of choice in making decisions about his life and his relationship with God, it is essential that our ability to think is not impaired. Temptation is great enough when we are in full control of ourselves, but when mind-altering substances are introduced into our systems, our ability to make wise and correct decisions is greatly decreased. Whenever our flesh gives in to the temptations of alcohol or drugs, we open a door for the devil and invite him in, because our defenses are down. I mentioned earlier about losing our inhibitions while under the influence of alcohol/drugs. Our sense of right and wrong becomes distorted. You can't hear the convicting voice of the Holy Spirit because the substance drowns it out. You may, however, genuinely feel the conviction when you sober up, but you quickly learn just how many drinks or how many pills it takes to drown out His voice again.

The truth is that the body of the believer is the temple of the Holy Spirit. When we abuse it in any way by the things we put into it, we are showing disrespect for His residence, not to mention the physical destruction that is taking place. How smart is that? How genuine is your desire to glorify Christ with your life? It is impossible for Christ to be glorified while something other than His Spirit has control over you. I understand that some people who are reading this may not even have a relationship with Jesus, and therefore do not have the Holy Spirit to help you in this area. You can pray right now to turn away from sin and to turn the control of your life over to Him and to accept His offer of forgiveness and salvation. And for Christians, who may not have victory in this area, remember that God is faithful and that there is no temptation stronger than you can bear. (1 Cor. 10:13) For those who may not have revelational knowledge of God's stand on this issue, search His Word. It is clear to me that He wants me under His influence at all times.

Prayer thought: Father, I know that this is a sensitive and sometimes controversial subject in Your body. How much of that controversy stems from Your children trying to rationalize a weakness in their lives? Help us, Lord, at all times to search Your Word for wisdom, for direction, and for Your perfect will. Help us to examine our behavior for the influence it has on others. Jesus, the blood that was shed on Calvary and the power that was released at the resurrection are stronger than any addictions the world has to offer.

Sharing My Body with God

"The body is not meant for sexual immorality, but for the Lord, and the Lord for the body." (1 Cor. 6:13b) "Flee from sexual immorality. All other sins a man commits are outside his body, but he who sins sexually sins against his own body. Do you not know that your body is a temple of the Holy Spirit, who is in you, whom you have received from God? You are not your own; you were bought at a price. Therefore honor God with your body."(1 Cor. 18-20)

Have you ever been in a bathroom where there were mirrors close to the bathtub? I don't know about you, but I personally don't like looking at myself unclothed. Why? Because there is just something about being naked that exposes all of your imperfections. You can't pretend they don't exist. Well, we all know that the Lord sees our nakedness every day, although sometimes we like to pretend that He doesn't. And by that, I don't mean just our physical body, but the whole of us, inside and out.

Our physical bodies are important to us and our physical bodies are important to the Lord. We have invited Him to live within us! He lives in us and through us. When we unite ourselves with Him, not only do our hearts belong to Him, but also so do our bodies. These verses say that our bodies become "the temple of the Holy Spirit". We have a permanent boarder taking up residence in our bodies. And I've got news for you. He doesn't take a vacation or go visit someone else for a few days or run out for a couple of hours so that you and your body can be alone for a while. He's always there, and if we are truly enjoying His presence in our lives the way we should, we will be glad that He is. It is His presence in our lives that should direct the decisions we make about how we use our bodies.

I like what verse 18 says about the temptation of sexual immorality. It says, **"Flee!"** That doesn't mean turn your head or walk away casually. It means "get out of there quickly!" The flesh is weak and God knows that it's only through grace, spiritual exercise, and a purposeful decision of our mind, will, and emotions that we can withstand those temptations. And the best way to resist the temptation is to get away from it. I used to tell my youth group when we were discussing this subject, "Don' t put yourself in a <u>place</u> to be tested." All sexual sins occur in a "place," whether it is a parked car, an empty house, a secluded room, etc. If you will avoid the <u>places</u> where the sin <u>could</u> take place, it most likely won' t take place. Most of us are wise enough to know what types of situations and circumstances lead to sexual sins. And if we <u>want</u> to or decide to before hand, we can avoid the situations and avoid the sin. We just have to learn to "flee." The good news is that we are not alone when faced with these temptations. Remember that you have a resident Helper within you in the person of Holy Spirit.

Prayer thought: Dear Lord, never let me lose sight of the fact that I am not my own, but have been bought with a price. Help me to remember that every decision I make concerning my body affects You because You reside within me. You know the temptations of this world concerning this issue, but Your Word also states that You will not let us be tempted beyond what we can bear and that for every temptation You have provided a way out. I can see clearly from these scriptures that the best way out is to "get out quickly."

Setting Sexual Standards

"But among you there must not be even a hint of sexual immorality or of any kind of impurity, or of greed, because these are improper for God's holy people." (Ephesians 5:3)

Sexual relations outside of marriage are sin, period, regardless of the gender of the persons involved, the age of the participants, or the circumstances of the encounter. For several years I was involved in teaching teenagers the principles of sexual purity before marriage through the "True Love Waits" program. It's easy for those of us who are adults to say that teenagers should not be having sex. It wasn't quite as easy for me to see, however, as a teenager growing up in the sixties. But do the same principles apply for "consenting" adults? And there are a lot of single adults, some divorced, some widowed, some never married. Sometimes adults seem to think that becoming an adult means that certain standards change in our lives. Eighteen or twenty-one becomes the "magic age" when certain things that you couldn't do as a child are now permissible as an adult. Wrong. Sin is sin. Age is irrelevant. God is consistent, and He doesn't change the rules. Oh, we recognize certain adult sexual sins as wrong. We certainly realize that prostitution and promiscuity are sinful lifestyles. But the sexual revolution of the last thirty years has softened our views on some sexual sins. We used to view living together outside of marriage as a sin. We now refer to it as "co-habitating." Society has even developed terms for these non-married, semi-committed partners. They are "significant others." And what about those who are married, but "separated"? And then there are those people whose spouses don't understand them, or leave them "unfulfilled." There is still a word for those types of sexual rationalizations…adultery.

The physical union we know as sex is a gift from God to be practiced within the marriage commitment. However, from the beginning of time, once this "gift" had been experienced, it began to be exploited. God didn't intend for man to have multiple wives, yet all through the Old Testament, we read of polygamy and extra-marital sexual relations…commonplace even among some of God's greatest men. And just as sexual sins have consequences today, many of them experienced the consequences of those sins back then. God intended human sexuality for man and woman to enjoy each other fully, to establish a means of procreation, and to establish the institution of the family. It was also meant to develop the physical idea of intimate, responsible, unselfish, devoted and committed love with another person that we could use as an example of the type of intimacy and devotion that God is looking for from us spiritually. When we exploit the gift, we exploit the Giver.

Prayer thought: Father, Your Word says that there is not to be even a "hint" of sexual immorality in my life. Satan has taken this good thing from You and so perverted it in this world that sexual relations outside of marriage have become a norm in our society instead of an exception. Lord, help us to return to the basic principles of Your Word. They were given to us not to confine or restrict us, but to protect us from the consequences of our sinful nature. In all sexual situations, help us to remember what is "improper" for God's holy people.

That Makes me So Mad! Now What?

"In your anger do not sin. Do not let the sun go down while you are still angry, and do not give the devil a foothold." (Ephesians 4:26-27)

Is anger a sin? It depends on how you respond to it. The emotion of anger itself is not a sin. How we handle it very often is. Paul addresses this issue quite succinctly in our focal verses today. The Holy Spirit-inspired words seem to recognize that anger is something we will be faced with. But there are clear instructions here not to allow your anger to result in sinful behavior. Anger is a breeding ground for sin. It can strike instantly like an erupting volcano, or it can fester and grow and erode silently like a cancer. How should Christians handle the inevitable circumstances in our lives that cause us to be angry? Maybe a more self-revealing question would be, "How have I mishandled anger in the past?"

The first thing that has to be done in any situation of our lives that may result in sin is to learn to recognize the danger signals that are about to push us over the edge. Learn your trigger points for anger. The devil knows them well. Some people have so rationalized their sinful angry behavior that they have accepted it as part of their character. "I have a very short fuse." "I'm just a hothead, I can't help myself." Repeated angry outbursts can become a part of your character only if you allow them to be. Does that mean that if I lose my temper occasionally that I'm not saved? Not necessarily. But if we do lose our temper and respond with verbal or even physical sinful behaviors, we should recognize it immediately as sin, repent, and ask forgiveness. Salvation results in a heart change, and a heart full of anger leaves no room for a heart full of God.

Our scripture today says, **"Do not let the sun go down while you are still angry."** That tells me that we are to deal with anger quickly. Think about this for a minute. When you are angry with someone, does it not affect other relationships in your life? How many of us have ever said or heard someone say to us, "I know you're upset, but don't take it out on me!" Anger will affect your relationship with Christ. We cannot truly worship the God who has changed our lives if there is a part of our life we are not willing to let Him change.

The question was asked earlier, "How do we handle anger as Christians?" Here are three steps that might help.

1) Recognize the warning signs in our own minds and bodies when they first begin to appear. Learn to do what works for us to keep anger from manifesting itself in outward signs of sin. Walk away, count to ten, pray, speak a scripture, start to sing…whatever works for you.

2) Take the initiative. If your anger is toward another person, you should be the instrument of reconciliation. Don't wait for the other party to make the first move, even if you are in the right. God can use these instances of reconciliation to strengthen the relationship beyond what it was before.

3) Settle it now. Unresolved anger is a dangerous and destructive thing. Issues are issues and there are workable solutions. They may not be perfect in the eyes of each party, but you may come to some agreements if you deal with conflicts before they get out of control.

Prayer thought: Lord, anger is an inevitable part of life, but please help me not to be controlled by it. Help me also, Jesus, not to justify or accept a "bad temper" as a normal part of my character. It is not Your character, so I do not want it to be mine. Help me, Lord, not to let anger fester and grow inside of me so that it interferes with my relationship with You and with others. By walking after the Spirit and not after the flesh, I will not let the devil have a foothold in my life in this area.

Heavenly 911

"Grace and peace to you from God our Father and the Lord Jesus Christ, who gave himself for our sins to rescue us from the present evil age, according to the will of our God and Father and to whom be glory for ever and ever. Amen." (Galatians 1:3-5)

There used to be a television program called "Rescue 911." My kids used to make fun of me as I watched it because I would always cry as the rescue was taking place. Even though the program' s main emphasis was on the rescue itself and the heroes and heroines responsible, there was always a feeling or sometimes even open statements of God' s presence in the situation. And a lot of the time (not always) a number of these life-threatening situations could have been avoided by better choices, people being more careful, wearing seat belts, paying attention to signs, etc. And so it is in our spiritual lives.

As I was studying for this lesson, I saw with my spirit' s eye a very large, high expanse of land, with a very steep cliff at the edge. Our entire life we are on that expanse of land slowing inching toward the cliff that drops off into eternal separation from God, or hell. Some stay on it longer than others do. Some stay out of the thorns and thistles along the way, and some get very tangled up in them. But each step, each day of our lives, brings us closer to the drop-off. How do we keep from falling off the edge of the cliff? Only one way. We have to call Heavenly 911. We have to call on the one and only Rescuer, the one and only Savior. We pray, we confess and repent, we ask Him to come, and He' s right there. The journey toward the edge of the cliff suddenly stops, and our course is changed. We have been rescued! (Caution: tears may occur at this point.) What a great source of hope! How did this Heavenly 911 system come to be?

Well, as in the case of the Rescue 911 system in place in our physical world, there had to be a plan, a vision for it. The organized rescue system we now take for granted in our daily lives was not always around. Before telephones, before para-medics, before helicopters, before the system of emergency rescue was established, many of the victims became fatalities. Somewhere along the line, someone had to have a vision of 911 and begin to take the first steps to put it into operation. That's where we are in today's spiritual lesson. God had a vision or an established plan of providing a Rescuer for His people. It would take a few years to put the whole thing together. But the good news is that He took the first step in establishing the plan one night in Bethlehem, and it came to completion thirty-three years later at Calvary. And what a perfect system it turned out to be! *"...for, everyone who calls on the name of the Lord will be saved." (Romans 10:13)*

Prayer thought: "Lord, how vividly I remember being on the road inching toward the cliff. Thank You, Jesus, for rescuing me! Help me, O God, to do all I can to let others know about Your rescue system. I see them every day. Some are tangled up in deception and confusion, and others are racing toward the edge at breakneck speed. Put me directly in their paths, Lord, for I have the information they need to reach their Rescuer.

Spiritual Work-Out

"We ought always to thank God for you brothers, and rightly so, because your faith is growing more and more, and the love every one of you has for each other is increasing.

Therefore, among God's churches we boast about your perseverance and faith in all the persecutions and trials you are enduring." (2 Thessalonians 1:3-4)

Why is Paul thanking God for his Thessalonian brothers in these verses? Verse three says that it is because there is evidence of their increasing faith and love for one another. Most of us realize that exercise is important for our bodies. Some take it a lot more seriously than others do. Think about exercise routines that you have established in your life or have observed in other's lives. If we do sit-ups, we are trying to firm up our stomach muscles. If we are involved in weight lifting, we are trying to develop stronger biceps or upper body strength. If we run or jog, we are working on our cardio-vascular system. And so it is with other areas of our body on which we are concentrating. As we regularly exercise these muscles, they become stronger. What happens if we do not exercise them? I would dare to say that most of us could look in a mirror, try to lift a heavy object, or try to walk up several flights of stairs and easily tell you the effects of the lack of exercise on our bodies.

So it is with our faith. Faith has to be exercised regularly to become stronger. Unexercised faith results in weaker Christians. All of us can testify that there have been times in our lives when we have been called on to carry heavy burdens. Most of us can also remember times when we've had a steep mountain of circumstances to climb. Those are the times we need to be able to flex our spiritual muscles and press on. The problem is that if we have not been on a regular spiritual exercise program prior to that time, our faith may be too weak to get the job done. The church is called the body of Christ. And just as our physical bodies need to be properly fed, nourished, and exercised, so does the body of Christ. We should also realize that the added weights in the training room, or the extra two miles we chart on the track, or the increased number of steps we choose to climb are designed to offer a purposeful resistance in our exercise routine to increase our strength and stamina. So it can be with the trials and circumstances of our lives with our spiritual workout. We can either choose to let them increase our faith by persevering or let them drain our faith by giving up. Paul was pleased with the exercise efforts of the Thessalonians. Is God pleased with ours?

Prayer thought: Father, it is my desire to remain spiritually fit. I know that means that I must commit myself to a regular spiritual exercise program of prayer, Bible study, and corporate worship. I also know that means that when resistance comes against me in the form of trials that I should view them as faith-builders. Increase my discipline to continue in spiritual exercise so that the end result is a strengthening of my faith and my inner man.

God Has It All Under Control

"All this is evidence that God's judgment is right, and as a result you will be counted worthy of the kingdom of God, for which you are suffering. God is just; He will pay back trouble to those who trouble you and give relief to you who are troubled, and to us as well. This will happen when the Lord Jesus is revealed from heaven in blazing fire with his powerful angels. (2 Thessalonians 1:5-7)

Our perseverance in times of trouble is <u>evidence</u> of God's <u>presence</u> in our lives. And God sees us and counts us worthy for it. And others see us and marvel. Have you ever been going through a really hard set of outward circumstances that everyone around you could see, i.e., a death of a loved one, an accident, a prolonged illness, loss of job, etc.? All you knew to do was hang on to God's hand a little tighter, and there was something about His touch that supernaturally strengthened you during that time. Unbelievers see our reaction during those times and stand in amazement at the strength and peace we display. They begin to question what their reaction would be to those same circumstances and very well may begin to question us about where it comes from. And all of a sudden we have an opportunity to share Jesus in the midst of our storm.

There is also a declaration in these verses of God's promise to take care of not only the problems but also the problem people in our lives. And He says this not so we can sit back and smirk and say, "God is going to get you for that," but so that we will not become pre-occupied with vengeful attitudes in our lives. We are to be pre-occupied with seeking God and His righteousness and trust Him to take care of the things that we cannot. And it is truly amazing how many times the giving over of those people who have wronged us to God ushers in a spirit of forgiveness in our hearts toward them. And that also can become a head-shaker for the unbeliever. "How can you let them get by with that?" Yet another opportunity to explain.

Most all of us know that although some of our trials seem frequent and intense, that for the most part they are short-lived, but for some they may be much longer. Part of the relief that God gives us during those times is through the Comforter who indwells us day by day through each minute of our trial. But Paul also talks here about the future relief that will come at the Lord's return. We have the assurance to know that both now and then, God's love will cover our problems. He has everything under control.

Prayer thought: Lord, what a comfort it is to me to know that by surrendering my life to You that I have released the control of circumstances and people in my life. Help me to remember that my perseverance during the storms of my life is an inward and an outward witness of Your presence in my life.

The Real Deal

"For the appeal we make does not spring from error or impure motives, nor are we trying to trick you. On the contrary, we speak as men approved by God to be entrusted with the gospel. We are not trying to please men but God, who tests our hearts." (1 Thessalonians 2:3-4)

As Paul writes here, he is answering charges that have been made against him by the Jews concerning his motives. The Jews were trying desperately to discredit Paul and his work because of his part in the spread of Christianity. If they couldn't get the people to discount the message, they would go after the messenger. The statements here in our focal verses are Paul's answer to these charges. Paul had to convince his Thessalonian friends that his love for God and for them was genuine in order for his ministry to continue to be effective.

"Christians" with impure motives can greatly damage the spread of the gospel. How many of us have ever wondered about the motives of someone offering to help us? Most of us who are parents know, or at least suspect, that if our kids volunteer to do something in the house that they usually run from, that they have either already done something they shouldn't have or they are trying to butter us up for something. Adults play those games, too. And most of us have been burned enough times in our lives by people with impure motives that we tend to be a little suspicious.

We all need <u>genuine</u> friends. We need those friends that we know are motivated by Christ's love for them and their love for Him and that shows itself true in their love for us. Friends that listen. Friends that give. Friends that help you fix your car, or your plumbing, or run errands, or baby-sit. Friends that genuinely care about you. Maybe they can't fix a bad circumstance in your life, but you know they're going to be there to go through it with you. Genuine friends who become the ears, hands, and heart of our most trusted genuine friend, Jesus Christ, are the kind of people He uses to draw others to Him. Friendship evangelism is one of the most powerful witnessing techniques that God can use to show people His character. It's our job to remain true to His character. It's our job to be genuine friends. That means we don't back out on our friends when they don't respond quite the way we think they should respond. That means we don't worry about "trade-offs." "I'll do this for you if you do that for me." That means we don't judge them or talk badly about them when they aren't around. It means we don't allow our lifestyle to become a contradiction to our profession of faith in Christ. How sad it is to hear an unbeliever make this observation about a believer, "If that's what it means to be a Christian, I don't want any part of it."

Prayer thought: Father, please purge my heart of all impure motives. I do not want to be the one who causes an unbeliever to doubt my genuineness. Lord, just as You entrusted the gospel to Paul and Timothy, I know that You have entrusted it to me. Help me to stay true to Your character and to develop <u>true</u> and <u>genuine</u> friendships based on Your love.

Specks and Planks

"Do not judge, or you too will be judged. For in the same way you judge others, you will be judged, and with the measure you use, it will be measured to you. Why do you look at the speck of sawdust in your brother's eye and pay no attention to the plank in your own eye?" (Matthew 7:1-3)

The O. J. Simpson trial was billed as "The Trial of the Century." We all watched, read, and evaluated the evidence. In the end, twelve people decided his fate. Thousands thought they were wrong. Thousands agreed with their decision. All of us set ourselves up as judge and jury. So who really knows? Mr. Simpson and God. Who is his final judge? The one with all the facts…God. On a smaller scale, how many of us set ourselves up as "judge" on a regular basis? We see someone do something or hear them say something, or worse yet, hear <u>about</u> something that has been said or done, and immediately begin to judge their actions, motives, and character. How many of us have ever misjudged someone? Think about that feeling we have after we discover we've misjudged them. How many of us have ever been misjudged? How do we feel toward the person who misjudged us? Misunderstandings cause a lot of misguided judgments. Depending on how close we are to the situation, most of the time we don't have all the facts, and we never truly know the attitude of another's heart. Yet, if we are not careful, we can easily become "conclusion jumpers." And an even sadder fact is that we like to bring other people around to our conclusion. And all because of a misunderstanding. There are also people who judge others to soften the character flaws and sin in their own lives.

I can remember very vividly God using this scripture in my life to change my attitude about judging others, and it was the part that says, "with the measure you use, it will be measured to you." As a youth leader I had lots of instances of young people sharing their hearts and discussing their problems. One student was having some trying times with another person. The problems seemed legitimate, and we spent time praying for restoration. There came a time when I received a phone call from the "other person." It was a pleasant-enough conversation, questions were asked and answered, opinions were discussed, and the conversation ended on what I thought was a positive note. I heard later that this person felt I was very rude on the phone. I didn' t intend to be rude, but my "judgment" of that person had been colored by my student' s stories and must have come across in that conversation. When the words came back to me that I had been "judged" a rude person, it hurt. The Holy Spirit led me to these verses in Matthew 7 and instructed me to read it every day for seven days. I did and these words hurt, but they come back to me now every time I am tempted to fall into the sin of judging others. I know I still do, but I'm a lot more conscious of it and a lot quicker to ask forgiveness for it.

The bottom line is that we have no business judging other people. We are all sinners; some of us are saved by grace, and some are desperately in need of it.

Prayer thought: Father, this world is like a glass fish bowl. We are constantly examining others and being examined by others. Help us to remember we are all swimming together. Lord, help us to be aware that misunderstanding can lead to wrong conclusions. Help us also to realize the damage that can be done to Your kingdom when Your children set themselves up as unqualified judges. Specks and planks, Lord. Quicken these words to my heart when this temptation enters my life.

Crash Landing

"But everyone who hears these words of mine and does not put them into practice is like a foolish man who built his house on sand. The rain came down, the streams rose, and the winds blew and beat against the house, and it fell with a great crash. When Jesus had finished saying these things, the crowds were amazed at his teaching because he taught as one who had authority and not as their teachers of the law." (Matthew 7:26-29)

This sounds very much like the passage before, except that the result is different when one word is added to the condition in verse 26. "...does not put them into practice." What result follows? We fall with a great crash. Sometimes it takes a few crashes in our lives for God to get our attention. But He's always there to pick us up and help us start the rebuilding process by saying, "Now, let's do it my way." How many of us have ever let a heart full of bitterness, anger, or jealousy result in an overloaded mouth that resulted in a destroyed relationship? If we had just prayed for the person (as Jesus instructed in chapter 5:43-48) instead of shooting our mouth off to him or about him, both his attitude and our own attitude about the situation would have probably changed.

How many of us have ever veered off the narrow path onto the broad road and wound up in the ditch? (Chapter 7:13-14) How about those who have made their jobs and the accumulation of material things the number one priority in their lives and then suddenly had their jobs taken from them? (Chapter 6:19-21) So Jesus is essentially telling us here that He has given us instructions on how to avoid some self-inflicted storms in our lives. If we fail to put them into practice, we are like the foolish builder. Not only that, but when the uncontrollable storms hit, we will have no foundation to which to cling. And the walls that we've built to keep the Lord at a distance will come crashing down around us.

By this time the crowds had gathered around Jesus as He was teaching His disciples. These were new teachings. These were real-life situations, not the regimented, impossible rules and regulations outlined by the religious leaders of the day. These were practices that could make a difference in people' s everyday lives. All of what Jesus was teaching here on this mountainside dealt with developing a life-style that would lead to better relationships with other people, the Lord, and ourselves. This was amazing stuff! I don' t think they realized at the time that these words were coming from the voice of God, just as surely as the Voice that spoke the Ten Commandments. But somehow they recognized that *"he taught as one who had authority."*

Prayer thought: Jesus, thank You for Your words of instruction. Thank You for caring enough about us to warn us of dangerous actions that may result in crash landings in our lives. Thank You that the Bible clearly reveals that You are the Son of God and that Your spoken words are true, authoritative, and powerful. Help us, Lord, to heed and to put into practice those things that You came to teach us.

Storm Warning!

"Therefore everyone who hears these words of mine and puts them into practice is like a wise man who built his house on the rock. The rain came down, the streams rose, and the winds blew and beat against that house; yet it did not fall, because it had its foundation on the rock." (Matthew 7:24-25)

We are going to talk about storms today. What are the characteristics of a weather-related storm? High winds, pelting rain, blowing snow, damaging hail, thunder and lightening, poor visibility. Storms may last a few hours or a few days, but for the most part they are relatively short-lived. We know when it begins that if we can just hang on, it will be over soon. But we also know that there are certain precautions we should take. I live in a tornado belt. I know if we are under a tornado watch that the weather conditions are conducive to their development. If we are under a tornado warning, I know there has been a tornado sited and that I should head for the basement level of my home. From experience, I've learned that when there is a lightening storm it would be a good thing for me to turn off my computer. Predicted heavy snowstorms send people running to the grocery stores for bread and milk. Hailstorms find me searching for a covered parking place for my vehicle.

Most of us have been through enough storms in our lives that we have developed patterns of reaction to them. We know that the best thing we can do in a storm is to protect ourselves the best way that we know how and just to ride it out until it's over. We wouldn't think about standing in the middle of the storm unprotected. Our instincts tell us to get inside or under something stable or firm that the storm can't shake. Yet many of us ignore those instincts when it comes to personal storms in our lives. And we all know that just as weather-related storms are periodic certainties, so are the personal storms in our lives. In our passage of scripture today, Jesus is just wrapping up the wonderful foundational teachings we know as the "Sermon on the Mount." And in this conclusion, He used an example that they could all relate to…storms. Jesus tells them that the things He has just taught will take them through the rough times. But He says just hearing these words is not enough. Our responsibility now is to put them into practice. Knowing the Word of God is not enough. We can go to church five nights a week and memorize hundreds of verses of scripture, but until we start <u>living</u> the Word of God, it is not going to become the foundation in our lives that will help us weather the storms.

Go back and re-read chapters 5-7 in Matthew. Let these foundational teachings become habitual practices in your life. Things like, "Do unto others as you would have them do unto you." "Judge not, lest you be judged." "Love your enemies." "Pray sincerely." "Blessed are the merciful." When we begin to put these things into practice, they will not only help us through the storms in our lives, they may actually head off a few storms that behavior contrary to these principles may bring about. And then search His word for His promises and learn to make them your place of refuge in the stormy times. During my own personal storms, I ran and stood on promises such as "I will never leave you nor forsake you," "Yea, though I walk through the valley of the shadow of death, I shall fear no evil, for thou art with me," "All things work together for the good of those who love the Lord and are called according to His purpose." What are you standing on in the storms of your life? ***"The rain came down, the streams rose, and the winds blew and beat against that house; yet it did not fall, because it had its foundation on the rock."***

Prayer thought: Lord, I know that the storms are going to come, but I thank You for Your Word that is my strong foundation. Father, thank You that You have provided a place of refuge for me. Thank You that You are my Rock.

Clean Heart Check

"Again Jesus called the crowd to him and said, 'Listen to me, everyone, and understand this. Nothing outside a man can make him unclean by going into him. Rather, it is what comes out of a man that makes him unclean.'" (Mark 7:14-15)

"He went on: 'What comes out of a man is what makes him unclean. For from within, out of men's hearts, come evil thoughts, sexual immorality, theft, murder, adultery, greed, malice, deceit, lewdness, envy, slander, arrogance and folly. All these evils come from inside and make a man unclean.'" (Mark 7:20-23)

Hypocritical Christians are a major stumbling block to bringing people to Christ. And don't think for one minute that just because you clean up the outside and do all the right "churchy" things that people aren't looking through you. People can see right through all that surface stuff. It's your heart and your life that is the true witness to Jesus Christ living in you. And not only do the people see it, God sees it. *(Mark 7:6b) "These people honor me with their lips but their hearts are far from me."*

Our second scripture reference today gives us a list of heart problems that Jesus wants us to examine ourselves for, or sin in our lives. It's not our hands that He is worried about being unclean, as is mentioned earlier in this chapter of Mark. It's our hearts. He gives us a list of heart problems here that lead to sin, which causes us to be "unclean," If you will notice, not all of the things on this list are action sins, some of them are attitude sins. Of course, attitudinal sin usually leads to a sinful action. Bad attitudes can put a dirty film on our hearts in a hurry.

Evil thoughts, sexual immorality, theft, murder, adultery, greed, malice, deceit, lewdness, envy, slander, arrogance and folly. This was the list that came to mind quickly as Jesus was exposing the hearts of the Pharisees. I'm sure there are many other actions and attitudes that we could think of that cause our hearts to be "unclean." Jesus was concerned here about the danger of attending only to the outside of ourselves, or the part that others see first and not worrying about those things we think we are hiding from people. I guess it is sort of like sweeping the dirt under the rug. He was telling the Pharisees, "If you're worried about being ceremonially clean before God, you've got to start from the inside out." How clean are our hearts? Are we allowing evil thoughts to creep in? What about greed? Envy? How about speaking in a derogatory or slanderous way about someone? Do your own check-list. Are there places we need to sweep completely clean? Are there places we definitely need to polish up? Or are there places we're going to need a bulldozer to excavate?

Prayer thought: Jesus, help me to stop and perform regular "clean heart checks" on my life. Expose those actions and attitudes in my life that have made me unclean. Help me to remember, Lord, that it is not just my Christian appearance that people are evaluating, but my Christ like-heart. Make me clean, Lord, from the inside out.

Buy Now, Pray Later

"For the love of money is a root of all kinds of evil. Some people, eager for money, have wandered from the faith, and pierced themselves with many griefs. (1 Timothy 6:10)

How many of us have ever listened to or watched a commercial for a big money lotto jackpot and found ourselves drifting into a fantasy of "Man, what I could do with 25 million dollars!"? The allure of wealth can be intoxicating. Because money is such a vital part of living, it is easy for it to become a driving force in our lives. We all need it to eat, to put a roof over our heads, to clothe our families, to own and operate a vehicle, for insurance and on and on. God promises to meet our needs. He has also given us instruction to work. If you are employed right now, even if it is not your dream job, stop and thank God for blessing you with that job. Sometimes, however, when unemployment comes or our needs are not being met like everyone else' s, we have to remember that God is still at work on a plan. And you have to ask yourself, "Am I doing my part?" Trust Him. ***"And my God will meet all your needs, according to His glorious riches in Christ Jesus." (Philippians 4:19)***

But be careful. Something happens when we are blessed with jobs or income sources that adequately or more than adequately meet our needs. We may start over-extending ourselves in the credit area, buying things that the world entices us with that we really can' t afford. Then all of a sudden, this job that God blessed us with to provide for our needs is not quite enough to pay the bills. Excuse my grammar, but that ain' t God' s fault! Then we find ourselves in a position of doing too much thinking about money, too much worrying about money, spending too much time devising ways to get more money, and we put God (and His tithe, ouch!) on the back-burner. Greed is said to be one of the seven deadly sins. And that could be because it snowballs so quickly. Therefore, as Christians we really have to be strong and stand firm in Christ in order to withstand the constant barrage of enticements to buy more than we can afford. It is very easy for us to be duped into thinking that we need more, bigger, better. There are just so many, "Buy now, pay later, low-easy payment plans" that will fit into a budget. Look at our focal verse again, *"...and pierced themselves with many griefs."* Anyone ever felt the grief of self-inflicted debt?

Now, just for the record, there is nothing wrong with having nice things. In fact, God wants us to live the abundant life. The rich young ruler' s problem was not that he had money, but that his money was more important to him than his eternal destiny. We just have to watch ourselves to see how much of our life is wrapped up in the accumulation of material things. God wants us to seek Him and his righteousness first, and all those things will be added to us. (Matthew 6:33)

Prayer thought: Lord, it is so easy in this world to get caught up in the rat race of chasing money and the things that it can buy. It starts out as need and turns to greed. Help me to examine my heart to uncover any unrighteous affection that I may have for making money, spending it, or accumulating it. Help me to be aware of the snare of the "debt monster" and to stay focused on seeking You.

Win or Lose...No Draw

"For whoever wants to save his life will lose it, but whoever loses his life for me and for the gospel will save it. What good is it for a man to gain the whole world, yet forfeit his soul? If anyone is ashamed of me and my words in this adulterous and sinful generation, the Son of Man will be ashamed of him when He comes in His Father's glory with the holy angels." (Mark 8:35-38)

In the evangelical Christian world we rely heavily on the words "saved" and "lost". When it comes to our eternal resting-place, you are either one or the other. There is no middle ground. Saved = heaven. Lost = hell.

Jesus talks about that in these verses. But even though salvation is a free gift and we don't have to work for it or buy it or earn it in any way, there is still something that has to take place. We "win" eternal life by receiving it, but then we have to start "losing" our old selves. It is in the "losing" of ourselves that we realize that we have received the saving grace of a transforming Savior. Jesus says if you want to "save" your life eternally, you have to "lose" your selfish life here on earth. You see, it's more than just a free pass to heaven. When you get saved, Jesus doesn't hand you a ticket and say, "Here you are. Now go do whatever you want, and then come back and get on the bus when you die." We have to let Him kill off the old "us," and most of us know that hurts sometimes. There are some things in our old nature that just seem to die hard. But there is an exchange that has to be made. In essence, Jesus is saying here, "Is hanging on to this old stuff really worth losing what I have to offer you eternally?" We have to let Him breathe into us this new life. Out with the old, in with the new! Die to self, live for Christ!

And then there is verse 38 in our focal passage today. "Do you really expect me to talk about Jesus or let people know that He is important? I'll stick out like a sore thumb. I have to live in this world you know!" *"If anyone is ashamed of me and my words in this adulterous and sinful generation, the Son of Man will be ashamed of him when He comes in His Father's glory with the holy angels."* That's enough said for me.

Prayer thought: Jesus, thank You for providing the way for salvation. Without You, Lord, we are all losers and destined to remain lost. Lord, thank You also that not only do You give us eternal life, but you also take away our old lives. But Lord, just as it is difficult sometimes for a baby to give up its bottle, a security blanket, or favorite toy, sometimes it's difficult for us to let go of things in our lives. Show us, Lord, that it is time to lay those things down and grow up! Oh, Jesus, help me never to be ashamed of You or what You have done for me! Help me to say like Paul, *"I am not ashamed of the gospel. It is the power of God for the salvation of everyone who believes..."*

How Much Is This Going to Cost?

"As Jesus started on his way, a man ran up to him and fell on his knees before him. 'Good teacher' he asked, 'what must I do to inherit eternal life?'....Jesus looked at him and loved him. 'One thing you lack,' he said. 'Go, sell everything you have and give to the poor, and you will have treasure in heaven. Then come, follow me' At this the man's face fell. He went away sad, because he had great wealth." (Mark 10:17, 21-22)

The rich, young man came to Jesus seeking something that he did not have. We find in these scriptures that he had great wealth. In Luke's account of this young man, we find that he was a ruler, so we know that he had position. But he must have been hearing about the teaching of this Jewish rabbi who was offering something that he didn't have. He sought Jesus out. "What must I <u>do</u> to inherit eternal life?" He had done all that everyone else had required of him. He had accumulated all there was that he desired to have. But he didn't have eternal life. Now from the account of this man's character in verses 18-20, we can assume that he was not an evil, heartless, ruthless, rich man. And one thing we should point out here is that being rich is not a sin. How wealth is handled or obtained is where so many fall prey to sin. This young man had a good heart and good moral standards. But he did have a sin problem.

Jesus looked in his heart and saw the love that this man had for the material things in his possession. You see, he had come to Jesus ready to do whatever it took to buy or earn eternal life, so he could add it to his list of possessions. He came looking only for the prize of eternal life. He didn't come looking for a relationship with Jesus Christ. <u>Eternal life apart from a personal relationship with Jesus is impossible.</u> Too many people are like the rich, young ruler in that they realize that this life is only temporary and they want to secure their place in heaven. They want the prize, but they don't want to have to give up anything. That in itself is a lie from the devil. Being a Christian is not a position of having things taken away from you. It's really a position of having more things given to you. It's just that your desires change, and you no longer want those things that hinder your <u>relationship</u> with the Lord. And when your relationship with the Lord becomes the driving force in your life, His blessings will be poured out on you in great measure. We've talked before about the concept of "losing" our old selves. Jesus wants to work out of us all of those things that we hold as more important than our relationship with Him. Think about it. He can't fill those places in our hearts with Himself if a controlling love for something else is there. But it is probably going to hurt when we first start letting Him weed out those things. Jesus looked into the heart of the rich, young man and saw that his love for material things and his position were the controlling loves in his life. Jesus, in essence, told the young man that he must lay that down to make room for Him. How did the rich, young ruler react? His face fell. He went away sad. He didn't get mad. He didn't try to buy Jesus off. He realized that for him the price was too high.

What about you? Is there a place in your heart that Jesus can't fill because something else is there? Are you seeking a relationship with the Savior, or just the prize of heaven? Is the price He is asking too high?

Prayer thought: Jesus, what is it that You are asking me to lay down in my life that is hindering my relationship with You? Your word says that You loved the rich, young ruler. I know that just as he was saddened by Your instruction, that You were saddened by his decision to walk away. Lord, help me remember that no matter what it costs me to follow You, it pales to the price You paid on Calvary.

From First to Last

"I am not ashamed of the gospel, because it is the power of God for the salvation of everyone who believes: first for the Jew, then for the Gentile. For in the gospel a righteousness from God is revealed, a righteousness that is by faith from first to last, just as it is written: 'The righteous will live by faith.'" (Romans 1:16-17)

There is no way to go out around the gospel for salvation. Paul didn't try to change it or water it down. The bad news is that all persons are sinners. Sin brings death and eternal separation from God. The good news (the gospel) is that Jesus, Who knew no sin, died on a cross for all sin, (mine, yours, his, hers, and theirs) and rose again on the third day. In so doing, He conquered death and provided for us the only way to be saved from an eternity in hell separated from God. And it is in the telling or the reading of that gospel story that the <u>power</u> of salvation is released to individual hearts and lives can be changed forever.

Who is the power of salvation released to? (***v. 16...everyone who believes***) The gospel was first given to the Jews, then the Gentiles. The gospel story reveals to us God's righteousness. We read of Jesus and His perfect walk in a far-less-than-perfect world. We know that He always made the right choices when confronted with some of the same temptations we are confronted with. We see the righteousness of God in Him. We can know right from wrong because it was revealed to us in Jesus, in the gospel story. When we believe by faith that His righteousness has been imparted to us, then we can begin to walk in it. That doesn't mean that we will always make right choices. It means that Jesus' righteousness has become our righteousness through the blood. But even though it doesn't mean that we will be perfect, you will notice in verse 17 that Paul talks about *"from first to last,"* which indicates a progression. We should constantly be striving toward making those choices that Jesus would make. <u>His</u> concept of right and wrong should become <u>our</u> concept of right and wrong. And it is our faith that should keep us going in the right direction.

Prayer thought: Jesus, by faith I believe that Your blood washed away all my sins. And I believe that when God sees me now, He sees Your righteousness. The power of my salvation gives me the power to walk in the righteousness You have revealed to me. Help me, Lord, constantly to be progressing and moving forward in that walk.

Love Walking

"Love must be sincere. Hate what is evil; cling to what is good. Be devoted to one another in brotherly love. Honor one another above your selves." (Romans 12:9-10)

Where do we start in our Christian love walk? We start in sincerity. How many of us, though, know that sincerity of the heart does not always translate into action? Good intentions do not always get the job done. How many of us are guilty of saying things and then not following through with them?

For example, "I'll call you sometime." "Let's get together for lunch." "I'll be praying for you." "I'll be there, if I can." "Call me if you need anything." Yet, we don't call. We don't go ahead and set a date for lunch. We don't show up. We see their need, but we wait for them to call us and hope they don't. All of a sudden our good intentions become very superficial and empty in the eyes of those to whom we've spoken them. Paul says, *"Love **must** be sincere."* And the reason it must be is that insincere love bears no fruit for the kingdom. In fact, it does more harm than good. And just as insincere people will impact the lives of others in a negative way, sincere people who go out of their way to demonstrate love will greatly impact the lives of others in a positive way. And as God's church, that is what we should be doing in the lives of both our own church family <u>and</u> the unchurched. We should be demonstrating love both collectively and individually.

Paul also talks here about hating what is evil and clinging to what is good. If we are going to learn to love as God loves, we also need to learn to hate what God hates…sin. We may say we hate sin, but do we? Too much of the world has seeped into most of our lives. We learn to ignore it, or sometimes even to tolerate it to the point of acceptance. We will be better and more sincere lovers of one another when we learn to <u>hate</u> gossip, jealousy, faultfinding, and strife. We will be better and more sincere lovers of one another when we learn to <u>cling</u> to kindness, patience, forgiveness, and true concern for each other's problems. Developing and practicing those things are first steps in walking out the love talked about in verse 10, ***"Be devoted to one another in brotherly love. Honor one another above yourselves."***

Prayer thought: "Lord, help me to cling to those things I know to be good. Convict me, Lord, when I am tempted to tolerate sin. Help me to discipline myself in following through with my good intentions and putting the needs of others above my own."

Is It Really Love?

"For God so loved the world that He gave His one and only son, that whoever believes in Him shall not perish but have eternal life." (John 3:16)

Our scripture today talks about something that is or should be at the very heart of our Christian walk. Love. "Love" is probably a word you use every day. We slap it in our conversations about everything from movies to hamburgers to hairstyles. Unfortunately, we throw it around sometimes too loosely in our relationships with other people. Relationships can become confusing or sometimes even shattered because the word "love" is easily spoken, but seldom demonstrated or even overtly contradicted by our actions.

We also know that there are different kinds of love. There have been thousands upon thousands of songs written about the love between men and women. We know that there is a special type of love between immediate family members. Most of us throughout our lives have had several people with whom we' ve developed special relationships whom we consider our very close friends. And, for the most part, we tend to think of love as an emotion, largely because when we think of it, we think about those people that bring our emotions to the surface.

But today we' re going to think about it as a conscious act of our will. Something that we purpose to do in our hearts for people; sometimes for people we know and sometimes for people we don' t know; sometimes for people who love us back and sometimes for people who don' t; sometimes for people who acknowledge our sacrifices for them and sometimes for people who don' t even recognize what we do for them. I'm speaking here about actively demonstrating love, not just talking about it. Genuine love. The real thing. Love that is identifiable in the eyes of the recipient. Love that does not expect something in return. The kind of love that we have received from God. The kind of love spoken about in the focal verse today. From His very own lips, as recorded in the gospel of John, Jesus spoke these words, **"...Love one another. As I have loved you, so you must love one another."**

That's a tall order. But throughout my walk with Christ I have found that He never asks us to do something that He is not prepared to equip us to do. One of the things that the Holy Spirit deposits in us when we become Christians is the supernatural ability to love as He loves. It is no surprise to me that is the first thing mentioned in the list of the fruit of the Spirit found in **Galatians 5:22**, and identified as the greatest attribute in **1 Corinthians 13:13.**

How's your love life? Is it all strictly surface or emotional? Is it highly selective? Or are you demonstrating the genuine love of Jesus Christ to the world?

"For God so loved 'the world'..."

Prayer thought: "Father, thank You for loving me. Forgive me for oftentimes taking Your love for granted. Show me how I might actively demonstrate Your love to others. Empower me, Lord, to walk daily in genuine love."

The Faith of A Child

"I tell you the truth, anyone who will not receive the kingdom of God like a little child will never enter it." (Luke 18:17)

I receive in the mail frequently, as I'm sure most of you do, envelopes announcing that I have already won, or am in the final ten, or could be the grand prize winner of…cars, large sums of cash, new homes, vacations, etc. And of course, there are always large, full-color photos of the prizes. And immediately the imagination kicks in and you start visualizing that car in your driveway, or phoning your work to resign because of your newly acquired wealth. But as you open the envelope, you'll usually find several strings attached. Things like forms that have to be filled out, or a telephone number to call for more information that usually involves a high-pressure sales pitch, subscriptions you have to buy, etc. And then as you read the fine print in an obscure part of the mailing, you'll see that the chances for winning the grand prize are something like 1 in 2,000,000. To be honest, I have filled out a few entries, but for the most part I decide quickly that it's not worth my time and effort, and they go right in the trash can. I have learned over the years that the world has nothing free to offer me. There are always high costs associated with its so-called prizes. Maybe that's why the concept of salvation being a free gift from God is hard for some people to take at face value.

Years of learning things the hard way, being taken advantage of, or a lifetime of empty promises breed skepticism and cynicism. We're not like that as children. In childhood, we lived in a world of trusting other people to supply our needs and to make us feel secure. For most of us, we were not concerned about paying for the groceries or the utility bill. We just had faith that when we got hungry there would be food in the kitchen and that when we were tired there would be a bed for us to climb into, and when our clothes got too small that we would get more. Jesus knows about the innocence and untainted faith of children and that's why He tells us in His Word that it is this type of faith that is necessary for all people, young and old, to receive salvation. All people need salvation and salvation is available for all people. You don' t have to fill out any forms. You don' t have to call a 900 number for more information. You don' t have to pay for it. You don' t have to beat the odds by having your name drawn from two million others. Those who put their faith and trust in Jesus Christ to forgive their sins receive salvation. Pretty simple…childlike faith.

Prayer thought: Thank You, Lord, for the gift of salvation offered freely to those who believe. Wipe out the skepticism and cynicism that creep into my life. Keep my faith innocent as that of a child. Help me to convey that faith to others who need to receive it.

Is Your Heart Showing?

"The Lord does not look at the things man looks at. Man looks at the outward appearance, but the Lord looks at the heart." (1 Samuel 16:7)

Outward appearances can sometimes be very revealing about a person's needs. We can usually tell a little bit about a person's financial needs by the outward signs: how they dress, where they live, what kind of car they drive, etc. We can see the hunger in the eyes of the children we see on television from other countries. Medical professionals can sometimes determine people's physical needs very quickly when they come into the emergency room bleeding or with broken bones. When we see someone crying, we see a need for comfort. Sometimes a person's spiritual condition is very obvious from the lifestyle he lives. But sometimes outward appearances can be very deceiving. We've heard stories, for example, of eccentric wealthy people who do not give the appearance of having money. We may also know people who give an impression of financial stability who are drowning in debt. In our hospital scene, we know that a lot of people come in with symptoms that are not quite so obvious, and they may need a number of tests run before the problem can be diagnosed and treated. And spiritually, there are a lot of people who give the outward appearance of being very good and moral who are just as "lost" as those people we have labeled "champion" sinners.

Outward appearances can lead to wrong assumptions. And in the body of Christ, sometimes that can be dangerous. I could assume that everyone who picks up this book is a believer desiring a daily devotion that teaches and strengthens his walk with his personal Lord and Savior, Jesus Christ. And for the most part, most of these teachings are written with that in mind. But someone may have picked up this book who is searching for something. You may not have a clue what it means to have a personal relationship with Jesus Christ, or even understand the term "salvation". Or you may have been "playing church" for a long time and may have done a pretty good job of convincing yourself and others that you are all right. I can't see your heart, but God does. Whatever your reason for reading these pages, whether it is for spiritual growth or for a spiritual discovery, my prayer is that you will allow the Holy Spirit to reveal the truth that is needed for your life.

We are going to be looking in the book of Romans for the next few days. Paul's letter to the Romans is a powerful look at what salvation is, who needs it, how to get it, and what happens to you after you receive it.

Prayer thought: Father, examine my heart. Do I need to strengthen my walk? If so, show me through Your Word the areas in my life that are less than what they should be. Do I even know You? Have I been fooling other people and myself with my outward spiritual appearance? Holy Spirit, reveal my spiritual condition to me.

I Have an Obligation

"I am obligated both to Greeks and non-Greeks, both to the wise and the foolish." (Romans 1:14)

What does it mean to be obligated? How many different ways can we be obligated? We can be obligated financially. We can be obligated in our relationships. Our time can be obligated to the commitments we have made. Actually, the word "obligated" carries with it sort of a negative connotation, because we view it as a reminder of something that has us bound up, in debt to, or constrained.

But if you think about it in another way, being obligated also means that you have received something of value. Paul knew that he had received something of tremendous value, his salvation. And he also knew that he had an obligation to his Lord to share that with the rest of the world. The Lord was not selective in his choosing of Paul, and Paul would not be selective with whom he would share the gospel. He would share with the Greeks, the non-Greeks, the wise, and the foolish. I suppose we would all fit in there somewhere. The bottom line is that even though Paul used the word "obligated" in this scripture, he did not see his obligation as a burden or something that he grudgingly had to do. He saw it as a burning desire of service stemming from love and gratitude.

How do we see our obligation to the Lord? How do we see our obligations to His church? How do we see our obligation to a lost world? Do we show difference in the people that we share Jesus with? Do we do the selecting, or do we let the Holy Spirit do the selecting for us? If you have received the wonderful gift of salvation, aren' t you glad that someone felt obligated to share with you? If you haven' t, read on, because this book is an expression of my own personal obligation to share my Jesus with you.

Prayer thought: Lord, remind me on a daily basis of the value of my salvation and the importance of my obligation to share it with someone else. Help me not to see it as a constraint on my life, but as an opportunity that You have given me to be a part of Your work.

Let's Work Together

"Just as each of us has one body with many members, and these members do not all have the same function, so in Christ we who are many form one body, and each member belongs to all the others." (Romans 12:4-5)

This is a down-to-earth, practical example of how the church is to operate. For the most part, we all know how the human body functions. And we know how each of our body parts does different things. There are a lot of people who have particular body parts that do not function correctly or who may even be missing body parts. We term these people "handicapped." Being handicapped in no way labels them as useless. There are many handicapped persons who have made enormous contributions to the world. But it does mean, perhaps, that they may need a little help in areas that a lot of us take for granted.

When my son graduated from high school, several families of seniors went together and rented the VFW hall to have a joint graduation party. As we were decorating, an uncle of one of the seniors was helping. He has been blind since birth. He was in charge of blowing up the balloons with the helium tank. We had blue and yellow balloons, and he had blown up several blue ones. At one point someone said, "That's enough blue ones; we need some yellow ones now." He replied, "Which ones are the yellow ones?" Oh, yeah. We forgot. So someone put a handful of yellow balloons in his shirt pocket, and there was no problem after that. He was very helpful. But naturally, there were some things the sighted could do that he couldn't do. By the same token, there were certain things that I couldn't do that called for a taller person or a stronger person. There was a lady in the kitchen working in food preparation who could make tomatoes look like roses. No one else could do that! But we all worked together, pooled our talents, gifts, and availability, and the party was a huge success.

So it is to be in God's church. Although you can get saved at home and never join a church, you most probably will not be the productive part of God's body that you could be if you would evaluate your spiritual gifts and put them to use where they are needed. If the body is to grow, all the members or the "parts" need to be active parts. And there are certain things that you can do that someone else cannot. Verses 6-8 in this chapter talk about a few of the giftings of God's people. Don't think to yourself, "I don't have a gift." The Bible says we all have gifts, different gifts, according to the grace given us. Some are more easily recognizable than others are. And that, to a large degree, is true because the recipient has exercised and developed his gift to the degree that it has become stronger and more apparent to others. If you are not sure of your gift or gifts, pray that God will reveal them to you. Another way is just to step in and try something new or something that you know you can't do without God's help. God blesses our willingness and our availability. You may try something for a while and find that it is not your area. Pray about that and see if God leads you in another direction. There is a danger, however, in bailing out too soon. Sometimes if we don't see results quickly enough from our efforts, we want to throw in the towel. I taught Sunday School for almost two years with only two or three "regulars," before God began to bring the harvest and the class eventually outgrew the walls and we had to change rooms. Sometimes God just wants to see how serious we are before He releases all of His power to us.

If you are already in a church and are exercising your gifts, talents, and availability in that body, praise the Lord! But, if you are not, either find a Bible-believing church or find a place in the church that you've been attending where you can become a productive body part. Serving God in His church should be a natural outpouring of our love for Him. It benefits Him, it benefits others, and it benefits us. As we serve God, we serve others, and others serve us. What a great plan! Surrender to God by praying, "Here I am, Lord. Use me." And then—jump in!

Prayer thought: Lord, I thank You for Your church, because Your Word says that it is Your body. And each one of us whom You have redeemed is a part of that body. Help me not to handicap Your body by withholding my gifts of service and usefulness. Show me, O God, my place of service in Your kingdom work.

Can I Pass This Love Test?

"Bless those who persecute you; bless and do not curse. Rejoice with those who rejoice; mourn with those who mourn. Live in harmony with one another. Do not be proud, but be willing to associate with people of low position. Do not be conceited." (Romans 12:14-16)

Here's a list of directives from Paul (inspired by God) that will test our love quotient. *"Bless those who persecute you."* But he didn't leave it at that. He went on to say, *"...bless and do not curse."* Retaliation is a major human defense mechanism. When we've been hurt, somehow we think we're going to feel better if the person who hurt us can hurt, too. When we've been undeservedly wronged or purposefully persecuted, our reaction is to defend or elevate ourselves by slamming the perpetrator. Being silent when under attack is not easy. Can it be done? Read the gospel accounts of Jesus' behavior while on trial in Jerusalem. Being silent is hard enough, but to actually say good things or bless those who hurt us is a little much to ask, isn't it? Read the words of Jesus on the cross. *"Father, forgive them for they know not what they do."*

The next directive in this passage is to rejoice with those who rejoice and mourn with those who mourn. Which is easier? What gets in the way sometimes of our rejoicing over someone else's good fortune? Jealousy or covetousness. The next time someone receives the promotion that you thought you deserved, or drives up in a new car that you'd love to own but can't afford, or wants to share with you any number of other joyful circumstances in his life, check your eyes for shades of green. Love testing.

Live in harmony with one another. That means somebody has to give in. That doesn't mean we are to compromise biblical standards or values. But, does it really matter sometimes where we go to eat, or who says he is sorry first, or whose turn it is for a particular job? Raising children is a real test of learning to live in harmony. Children have a really good memory and a quest for "fair." I think that my son, who is my middle child, must have kept a notebook of all the things his older sister received or was allowed to do at certain ages. Although there were four years separating them (enough time for his memory to fade), it was amazing how many times he would announce to me at various age levels, "When Sarah was my age, you let her do this, go there, buy that, etc." And if the present circumstances in his life didn' t warrant the same decision at that time, then I wasn' t being fair. Teaching children that life isn' t always "fair" may save them some major disappointments later in their lives. Too often we take the "that' s not fair" attitude with us into adulthood. Learning to sacrifice our own way for the sake of harmony is a big step in demonstrating our love walk.

Do not be proud. Do not be conceited. Do not limit our witness or our associations with those who are the most like us. Genuine love crosses racial, social, economical, and religious lines. Most of us gravitate toward those people with whom we have the most in common and there is nothing wrong with that, unless we make it a barrier in getting to know and love others who don' t "fit" our mold.

Prayer thought: Jesus, these are some very practical, everyday instructions for walking in Your love. But, Lord, You know how difficult they are. I'm not sure I can pass all of these love testings. Help me to recognize them as they show up in my life as opportunities to strengthen my love walk and to act and react from what You' ve taught me here.

Who Do People See When They Look At Me?

"Be imitators of God, therefore, as dearly loved children and live a life of love, just as Christ loved us and gave himself up for us as a fragrant offering and sacrifice to God. But among you there must not be even a hint of sexual immorality or of any kind of impurity, or of greed, because these are improper for God's holy people. Nor should there be obscenity, foolish talk or coarse joking, which are out of place, but rather thanksgiving." (Ephesians 5:1-4)

Imitators of persons are people who take on the speech patterns, mannerisms, and characteristics of other persons to such a degree that they become easily recognizable as the person they are imitating. We've all seen people in the entertainment industry who imitate well-known people. And depending on how well they have perfected their portrayal of the other person, we usually laugh or remark on how much they sound or look like the famous person. But the concept of imitating God is not to be taken light-heartedly or for the purpose of entertainment. Genuine Christians who love the Lord begin to take on His characteristics. Don't set your goal as a Christian on trying to emulate or imitate another Christian. Set your goal on imitating Christ. Christ's character consistently demonstrates love. Love is the key to consistent Christian behavior. Agape love changes you from the inside out. That type of love will break out in your thoughts, words, and actions, and people will begin to see more of Christ and less of you.

If that is to happen, we have to start removing some things in our lives that are not consistent with the Person we are trying to imitate. My kids know that I do not like trash lying around. And one of my favorite and most consistent lines is, "Why is it that I'm the only one around here that can see this mess?" To which they reply, "What mess?" As a Christian we have to start recognizing the trash in our lives, and we have to start dealing with it. I said earlier that agape love, or the unconditional love of Christ, changes us from the inside out. And one of the ways it changes us is by our tolerance level of sin. If we are going to be imitators of God, we cannot live like the rest of the world. <u>A big part of</u> our "conversion" is our sudden "aversion" to sin. That' s not to say that once we become a Christian, we are never going to sin again. It just means that we are not going to like it when we do. We will recognize it for sin, repent, ask forgiveness and remove it from our lives. We are not going to want to remain in a consistently sinful lifestyle. Persons who consistently live in sinful lifestyles that they have rationalized or learned to accept as part of their character are not striving to imitate Christ, and have not experienced the transforming grace of God. (Read verses 5-7 in our selected passage for today.)

Examine your life. Do you need a house cleaning? Is there trash in your life that needs to be removed? Can you even see the mess? Even if you can' t see it, you can be sure that other people can. Do people see Jesus when they look at you? If not, maybe you need to work a little harder on your imitation of Him.

Prayer thought: Jesus, help me to keep my house clean. Open my eyes, Holy Spirit, that I might see the trash in my life that keeps people from seeing You when they look at me.

I Have Been Called

"I myself am convinced, my brothers, that you yourselves are full of goodness, complete in knowledge and competent to instruct one another. I have written you quite boldly on some points, as if to remind you of them again, because of the grace God gave me to be a minister of Christ Jesus to the Gentiles with the priestly duty of proclaiming the gospel of God, so that the Gentiles might become an offering acceptable to God, sanctified by the Holy Spirit." (Romans 15:14-16)

This is Paul describing the call on his life. What was it? It would seem that he was acknowledging that God had called him to be a minister of Christ Jesus. This was the apostle Paul…fervent, zealous, mighty man of God. The call on his life was to be a minister of Christ Jesus. Come to think of it, that's the call on my life as well. And if you are a Christian, it is the call on your life also.

Even though Paul would tell anyone who would listen about his wonderful Lord and Savior, Jesus Christ, he felt that he had a specific call to reach the Gentiles…meaning anyone who was not a Jew. Sometimes some of us feel that we have a specific call or are more led to minister to certain groups of people, at least during certain seasons in our lives. For example, there was a period of ten years in my life when I felt my strongest calling was in the area of reaching teenagers. I was the youth leader in our church at that time and invested a lot of time and energy into the lives of dozens of teenagers during those years. I saw many of them come to know Christ as their Savior and a few of them, including my own son, surrender their lives to the ministry. And it was nothing that I did, but it was something that God did through my willingness to recognize and to walk in the specific calling on my life for that group of people.

There was another young man in my Sunday School class, who is now a pastor, who felt a call on his life to reach those who are trapped in the world of alcohol and drugs. Having been delivered from that world himself, he knows all the twists and turns on that road that can lead to destruction. There may be others who feel led to minister to children, or to senior citizens, or the homeless. Some feel a call of foreign missions on their lives, to go and share the gospel with an unreached people group.

How about you? Is there a certain group of people that God is sending you to reach? Maybe it's your family. Or how about the people you work with? Look around at your circle of influence. Where has God placed you? Are there hurting people there? Are there lost people there? Is there a road that you have traveled that others are traveling now that perhaps you could help by sharing your experiences of God's grace? Paul said, "I myself am convinced, my brothers, that you yourselves are full of goodness, complete in knowledge and competent to instruct one another." Close your eyes and say out loud to yourself, "He's talking about me."

Prayer thought: Father, just as You called Paul to reach the Gentiles, I know that You have called me to reach someone else, or perhaps a group of people. Show me those people, Lord. And then, help me to recognize, accept, and walk in that calling.

Do You Want To Hear Something Really Good?

"Then leaving her water jar, the woman went back to the town and said to the people, 'Come see a man who told me everything I ever did. Could this be the Christ?' They came out of the town and made their way toward him." (John 4:28-30)

One Sunday morning I walked into the classroom noticeably excited and obviously enthusiastic about something. I proceeded to tell the class, "I received such wonderful news this week. It just came right out of the blue, totally unexpected. I was so overjoyed that I cried for a minute and then I started laughing, and I still just can' t believe that it is really true. I'll probably be enjoying this feeling for a long time. I had received a phone call from someone and I remember thinking after they had hung up, 'What if I hadn' t been home when they called. Would they have called back or would they have called someone else?' I just blocked that out of my mind. I did receive the call and I still can hardly believe it." At that point I began to change the subject and directed us into prayer time by asking for any praise reports or prayer requests. They would have none of that. "What happened?!!" "Who called?!" "What was it?!" My response was, "My good news? Oh, you probably wouldn' t be interested. It wouldn' t mean as much to you. I just don' t think I could share it with you. It was sort of personal." I was met with stares of disbelief and confusion.

Then I confessed. This was cruel and unusual punishment. There was no phone call. And by this time you' ve probably already guessed that the lesson today revolves around our telling the world about our experience with Jesus Christ. People who view our lives should be able to see the joy, excitement, peace, contentment, and hope in our lives that demands an explanation. If we are living the way we should, we should detect the same "eagerness" in their faces that I saw in the faces of the students of that Sunday School class that morning. But in order for me to evoke that kind of response from that class, it was up to me to get their attention and move them to the point of asking questions. So it is in our daily encounters with the lost world. Whether consciously or unconsciously our lives should be attention-getting to the point of evoking response. Maybe at first it is just curiosity, but then an eagerness to know "why, how, what, or who" has caused us to be the way we are. What we have is not a secret, although some Christians seem to think they should keep it to themselves. The woman at the well dropped her water jar and ran back into town to tell about her encounter with Jesus. I would assume that she made a big-enough scene there to command some attention. The result? ***"They came out of the town and made their way toward him."*** That is the same result we should be seeking.

Prayer thought: Lord, am I really excited about my relationship with You? Is it showing? Help me, Jesus, to live my life so that the joy of my salvation is ever apparent, so that it grabs the attention of the lost and opens up doors for me to share the wonderful good news of the gospel.

Take My Name...and Use It!

"Then Jesus came to them and said, 'All authority in heaven and on earth has been given to me. Therefore go and make disciples of all nations, baptizing them in the name of the Father and of the Son and of the Holy Spirit, and teaching them to obey everything I have commanded you. And surely I am with you always, to the very end of the age.'" (Matthew 28:18-20)

The setting here is during that period of forty days after the resurrection and before the ascension as Christ appeared in his resurrected body. For thirty-three years God Himself had walked on the earth in the physical body of Jesus Christ, walking, talking, thinking, acting, reacting, and living perfectly before men, especially twelve men. And especially in those last three years, he lived before them not as a performer or someone to be marveled at, but as an example or goal of living for them and for all of us.

They had experienced the touch of Jesus in their lives. They had seen the perfect way to live and the relationship He had with the Father. They had developed a relationship with Him that would forever change their lives. Now, Jesus was telling them that there was going to be a transference of power to them so that they might impact people in the same way that He had impacted them. He was leaving them that authority through the power of His Name. They couldn't do what they had to do in the power of their own names, but only when they went in His. **"Therefore...",** He said, **"go forth and make disciples of all nations, baptizing them in the Name of the Father and of the Son and of the Holy Spirit, teaching them..."** It doesn't start with baptism. It starts when we begin a personal relationship with the risen Savior. It doesn't stop with baptism. We do not become disciples simply by getting wet, although baptism following conversion is important, as it becomes a testimony of our new lives in Christ. We become disciples by being discipled ourselves and by being taught how to disciple others. And Jesus ended this directive with an encouragement, "I will always be here. You are not alone."

The New Testament churches became our models for believers who were living in a common geographic area to congregate and bind together to work as a team to reach the lost in their communities. And from these small gatherings of obedient believers, we saw and continue to see the multiplication process of the kingdom as the geographic areas began to stretch. Can you be counted among those who can say, "Thank God that it stretched to me?" Evangelizing the world is a major task. But look how far it has come from twelve men who took Jesus seriously enough to become "Great Commission Christians".

Prayer thought: Jesus, I thank You for giving me Your Name and the power to use it to bring others into relationship with You. Strengthen me and my local church, Lord, to stretch our boundaries, to go, and to make disciples of all nations. And thank You, Jesus, for the promise that we take not only Your Name and Your power, but that You personally walk beside us every step of the way, even to the ends of the earth.

Bringing "Outsiders" Inside

"Be wise in the way you act toward outsiders; make the most of every opportunity. Let your conversation be always full of grace, seasoned with salt, so that you may know how to answer questions." (Colossians 4:5-6)

People everywhere, Christians and non-Christians, have strong tendencies to associate with people who are like them. We like to be around people with whom we have something in common. It makes for better conversations and relationships. But all of us come into contact from time to time with "outsiders." God will see to it. These are people we don't really know or people who are totally different from us. Paul says, *"Be wise in the way you act toward outsiders; make the most of every opportunity."* Of course, we can assume that he is not talking here about other Christians who may go to another church. Although sometimes I have seen God's people treat fellow believers from other Christian denominations as "outsiders." Paul is referring to those "outside" the faith. Specifically, he says to take advantage of every opportunity that you may have to show Jesus, either in word or deed, to someone who is still lost or separated from God by his sin.

Let's be realistic. Not only would it be impossible and most likely ineffective, but also could even prove to be counter-productive, to walk up to every stranger in the mall or at a football game and try to present him with the plan of salvation. What Paul does tell us in today's passage is that in our conversations with people, we should let our words be full of grace. Let our faith and our love and our stand for Christ be apparent. *"Let your words be seasoned with salt, so that you may know how to answer everyone."* If you don't know exactly what to say to somebody, go slowly. Think before you speak. Wait for the Holy Spirit to direct you. Let your conversation with them be pleasing and interesting and just salty enough to keep them thirsty. Your attitude with them is extremely important. That means to be genuinely concerned and interested in what they have to say. If you expect outsiders to be brought "inside" the family of God or to become Christians, your attitude had better let them know it's a good thing to be.

Pray for divine appointments with "outsiders." God will give them to you. Learn to recognize them, and to take advantage of every opportunity.

Prayer thought: Jesus, as I was writing this, I was reminded of Your divine appointment with an "outsider," the woman at the well. You had nothing in common with her socially or intellectually; yet your conversation with her drew her into Your circle. Help me, Lord, to recognize my responsibility to draw the outsiders inside.

Getting Involved

"Tychicus will tell you all the news about me. He is a dear brother, a faithful minister and fellow servant in the Lord. I am sending him to you for the express purpose that you may know our circumstances and that he may encourage your hearts. He is coming with Onesimus, our faithful and dear brother, who is one of you. They will tell you everything that is happening here." (Colossians 4:7-9)

There seems to be an increasing fear or aversion in our society of getting involved in the lives of others. Satan has convinced us that by spending too much of our time and energy ministering to others that we are detracting or subtracting from our own lives. Let's face it, some people are very high-maintenance, meaning they have issues in their lives that require a lot of attention. So, it is much easier to send those people to the pastor, pastoral staff, or deacon body to have their needs met. "After all," we think, "they have a lot more time to deal with them than we do, and besides that's their job." If that happens too often, however, you can see how soon the church leadership would have no time for anything else.

You can see in our scripture passage today, that Paul, being unable to physically minister to the people in this church, sent others who were lay people to minister to them. These are not "big names" in the Bible, but you can be assured that they are big names in the kingdom. Perhaps they didn't make the impact on recorded Christian ministry that Paul did, but it is highly likely that they made an impact on individual lives of that time. And that's what we are called to do…to impact lives for Christ. And that is going to require "getting involved" in people's lives. Paul couldn't be everywhere at once. Paul couldn't personally minister in depth to all those who heard him preach. But he was always interested and always concerned about the body as a whole and the body as individuals. He was building spiritual helpers along the way to invest in the lives of God's people. And that's the job of the leaders in our churches today. Pastors, elders, and deacons minister <u>and</u> train others to minister. Teachers minister and train others to minister. Think back in your life about the person who was most responsible for showing Christ to you. It may have been a church leader, but it very well could have been someone who specifically took time for you, to listen and share and to get involved in your life.

Just as there is a danger of over-involvement in the lives of pastors and leaders, we have to be sensitive to that danger in our lives. If we try to take on too many people's personal ministry needs, soon we will become over-burdened and ineffective in the lives of the ones that God has specifically assigned us. Soon we become overwhelmed and frustrated, throw up our hands and back away from everybody. Over-involvement leads to under-involvement. That's why it is good that God keeps growing up more Christians. If each of us can consistently become personally involved in the life of someone else and invest the quality time that is required with that individual, we will start making progress in the kingdom because then we will see those individuals model our example in the life of someone else.

We also need to be sensitive to the Holy Spirit when He lets us know that it's time for us to increase or decrease our involvement with a particular person. If we look back on our lives, most of us can think about people who were a major part of our lives for a while but, through circumstances have assumed, a lesser role. For example, a good friend of mine who is in the medical field had another good friend who was diagnosed with breast cancer. For a period of several months most, of her spare time was devoted to "being there" for that friend. Leigh's medical skills served as a benefit to the woman as she helped with changing dressings on her surgical site. And Leigh's knowledge helped to calm the friend by being there to answer questions as they came up. But Leigh also spent a lot of time just being a shoulder and a dependable presence in the woman's life. After a time, the recovery took place, and that season of concentrated ministry for Leigh was lifted, and since then she has been given many others to focus on, usually one or two at a time. Does that mean that she has totally left behind that relationship with the first friend? No, it just means that we have seasons of focus. God shows us the hurting or searching people that He is placing in our lives through circumstances. And these circumstances should lead to our getting involved or investing in their lives. This type of investment reaps a great return.

Prayer thought: Lord, help me never to back away from the needs of people. Don' t let me get by with surface or easy involvement, like putting a little money in an offering plate for a hungry person, or calling the pastor when I hear about someone who is sick or struggling with an emotional problem. I understand now that You want me to get involved personally in their lives. As I build more and more personal relationships with the lost or hurting people of this world, the better chance there is for them to develop a personal relationship with You.

Anybody Hungry?

"Blessed are those who hunger and thirst after righteousness, for they shall be filled." (Matthew 5:6)

How many of us have ever been hungry and didn' t really know what we wanted to eat? I would say that most all of us have had that sensation. Nothing really sounded good. We just knew we had a hunger that needed filling. And we just knew that food of some kind was a substance that would take that hunger away. But no matter how "stuffed" you might feel after feeding that hunger, in a few hours that sensation wears off, and we're back in the kitchen opening refrigerator and cabinet doors searching again.

This physical concept of unfulfillment carries over into our spiritual lives. All people have a spiritual appetite even if they don' t recognize it. All we know is that we are hungry. All we know is that there is something empty inside that needs to be filled. We know we want or need something, but we just don' t know what it is. If we are not pointed to the source of our fulfillment, Jesus Christ, many of us begin to try to fill that emptiness with worldly things. And a lot of those things are very bad for our spiritual diets: alcohol, bad relationships, drugs, materialism, self-gratification, self-glorification, etc. Sometimes the worldly things we try to fill our lives with are not "bad" things, but may even be considered "good" things, like family, education, careers, causes, good works, or even religious activities. For some reason, though, all of them leave us unfulfilled inside. We have to come to the point individually when we realize that the worldly things we thought would fill us do not really satisfy the emptiness we have inside. It' s an emptiness that is very hard to describe. But we have to get to the point where we know that we need something more.

Then the question is "How do I get it?" When people start recognizing this need in their lives, that is when the Holy Spirit can start pointing them to the source. As Christians, it is very important that we become sensitive to that timing in case He wants to use us as a pointing instrument. Timing is important. How many of us have tried to spoon feed a baby who wasn' t hungry and especially didn' t want those mashed carrots? You can play airplane in the hanger, eat "yummy" spoonfuls yourself, or stand on your head and whistle, but until he opens his mouth, you' re not going to get it in. Sometimes Christians don' t understand why non-Christians don' t "see it" the way we do. Really, we try to cram too much in them at once, but until they are ready to receive it, we won' t get very far. We may get the gospel "on" them, but we won' t get it "in" them. The only thing that can fill the spiritual void inside of us is a true relationship with Jesus Christ. We can' t fill that part of us with anything else that will last. Jesus describes Himself in many places in the Bible as the "Bread of Life", and the "Living Water." Jesus is our eternal substance for eternal sustenance.

Prayer thought: Father, I remember the initial hunger in my life for that "something" I was missing. Thank You, Lord, for providing me with the Bread of Life. Jesus, now that I recognize how fulfilling my life with You can be, I pray that my spiritual appetite stays sharp and that I recognize my need to stay hungry and thirsty for the things You want to teach me.

It All Makes Sense Now

"Then He opened their minds so they could understand the scriptures. He told them, 'This is what is written: The Christ will suffer and rise from the dead on the third day, and repentance and forgiveness of sins will be preached in His name to all nations, beginning at Jerusalem. You are witnesses of these things.'" (Luke 24:45-48)

After the resurrection, Jesus began appearing to people. He appeared to Mary at the tomb. He appeared to the two walking on the Emmaus road. Our focal verses occurred as Jesus appeared to His disciples as they were gathered together talking about the events of the last few days. His appearance startled them, but as He began to speak, suddenly the pieces started to fit together. All the words of the prophets and the spoken words of Jesus not only came into their remembrance, but now began to make sense. And I think that is why Jesus was so patient and understanding with them up until this point. Until the disciples had seen, heard, and experienced all of this, they just couldn' t understand the scope of it all. But now, as He stood before them, raised from the dead, He opened their minds that they might understand. And they did. Isn' t that a lot like us? We can witness and explain to people until we are blue in the face, but until they come face to face with the truth of their own lost condition and realize that they don' t want to remain that way, the scriptures won' t really make any sense. And when they reach the point of awareness, the Holy Spirit steps in and opens their mind to gospel.

Jesus was basically saying to His disciples and us, "It' s your turn now. You' ve seen, you' ve heard, you' ve experienced the power of the resurrection. I didn' t go through this for the few of you gathered in this room (although He would have), but the message of repentance and forgiveness is available to all, and it must be preached to all." The impact of the resurrection didn' t stop with a few hundred people to whom Christ appeared before His ascension. Had it not been real, the story could not have survived. It has not only survived, but has intensified over the last 2000 years. It probably would have been given a few lines in the history books and maybe even been relegated to "The Legend of the Empty Tomb." But because of the faithfulness of the believers, of those of us who have experienced a personal, living, vibrant relationship with this man the Jews tried to eliminate, we know Him to be "the Christ, the Messiah, our Savior, our Reconciliation with God the Father." And day after day, year after year, people responding to His words, "You are witnesses of these things," continue to bring others to a saving knowledge of Him.

Some questions need to be asked here. Have you responded to the empty tomb by repenting of your sins and accepting the forgiveness offered on the cross? Have you experienced the power of the resurrection by believing that Jesus rose from the dead to give you eternal life? If so, are your life and words a witness to these things?

Prayer thought: Holy Spirit, thank You for opening my eyes to the truth of the gospel. Thank You, Lord, for the revelation that Bible stories are not just stories. It all fits together and the more I study it, the more You illuminate it to me. Lord, help me to demonstrate and vocalize it to those around me.

In the Right Place at the Right Time

"While they were wondering about this, suddenly two men in clothes that gleamed like lightning stood beside them. In their fright the women bowed down with their faces to the ground, but the men said to them, 'Why do you look for the living among the dead? He is not here; he has risen! Remember how He told you, while He was still with you in Galilee: The Son of Man must be delivered into the hands of sinful men, be crucified and on the third day be raised again.' Then they remembered His words."(Luke 24:4-8)

Most of us have experienced the death of a relative. You know that there are certain things that have to be done. You have to make the "arrangements," like calling the funeral home, choosing people to conduct or participate in the service, and setting times for visitation and the funeral. It's a busy two or three days. And I guess that is a good thing as it keeps the mind occupied with things that have to be taken care of so you don't have time to dwell on the emptiness you feel. The women spoken about in this passage loved Jesus very much. What they had just witnessed was very traumatic for them, yet there were certain things that had to be done after a death. The body was to be anointed with spices, and somebody had to do it. Because of the observance of the Sabbath, however, they were not allowed to be out and about until it was over. So they went to the tomb early in the morning to anoint the body.

What do you think those women felt when they saw the stone rolled away? What do you think they felt when they entered the tomb and found it empty? I would expect there were a whole gamut of emotions; fear, anger, confusion, wonder, despair…because, at this point, the possibility of resurrection had not occurred to them.

And God, in His infinite wisdom, knew the state of mind these women and the rest of Jesus' followers were in. He didn't leave them to wrestle with the question all by themselves. He had someone strategically placed at the tomb to give them the good news. And, praise God, He does the same for us today. Left to wrestle with our own sin problem and need for a Savior on our own, some of us may not have come to the correct solution on our own. God is still using messengers to spread the good news. Even though the angels told the women, "He's not here. He has risen," and then reminded them of the words Jesus Himself had spoken about this day, they still did not completely understand…but it was a start. And that's the way it is with us today. Jesus strategically places people in the right places at the right times to point us to Himself. Sometimes it is with a direct spoken word, testimony, or a sermon. Sometimes it may be an act of kindness, mercy, or compassion shown by an indwelt believer. It may be through consistent observance of the Christian lifestyle of a person whom God has put in our life.

And we do not have a full understanding at first…but it is a start. How about you? Who was there for you in the right place at the right time? Why don't you take a minute right now and thank God for His messenger. Has God ever put you in the right place at the right time to proclaim the good news? Have you been obedient in those times? Don't let those opportunities pass. The news is too important! He is risen!

Prayer thought: Thank You, Lord, for that person You placed in my life at just the right time. Thank You for preparing my heart to hear and receive the good news. Jesus, I am asking for divine appointments. I am asking that You place me in the right places at the right times to share the good news with someone else. And prepare their hearts, God, to receive it.

Easy Does It

"As apostles of Christ we could have been a burden to you, but we were gentle among you, like a mother caring for her little children. We loved you so much that we were delighted to share with you not only the gospel of God but our lives as well, because you had become so dear to us." (1 Thessalonians 2:6b-8)

Paul said, *"We were gentle among you, like a mother caring for her little children."* In my reading of Paul's writings, "gentle" would not be the first word that comes to my mind in describing him. I see him with a very bold, natural personality. But there is also enough evidence of his character in scripture to know that he was a man who walked after the Spirit of God. And gentleness is a part of the fruit of that Spirit. (Galatians 5:23) I am sure he was bold when the occasion called for boldness and gentle when it called for gentleness.

In most instances in our daily encounters with people, there is no need for us to be harsh and domineering. There is a phrase often used in witnessing techniques that says, "We don't win people to Christ by beating them over the head with our Bibles." One of the things that I regularly ask of the Lord is to soften and sweeten my spirit. Sometimes it is the gentle touch that goes the farthest with people. Think about it. If there were to be a loud, abrasive horn blast go off in the room, most of us would cover our ears to block out at least part of the undesirable sound. But if someone in the room with us were to lower his voice to a whisper and ask us to pay close attention, we would get very quiet and strain to pick up every word. We are to display the character of Christ, and Jesus describes His gentleness in Matthew 11:29 *"Take my yoke upon you and learn from me, for I am gentle and humble in heart, and you will find rest for your souls."*

Paul goes on in our focal verses today and says that he and his friends not only shared the gospel with the Thessalonians, but their lives as well. And as we get to that point and begin to share our lives with one another, the Holy Spirit can begin to effect the life changes in <u>us</u>

that He desires, as well as in those with whom we are sharing. Reread verse 8. What caused Paul and his friends to respond to the Thessalonians in the manner they did? *"We loved you so much,..."* Are we loving each other much? Do we truly love the people we are trying to win to Christ? If we don' t, we will probably just share the words out of obedience, or maybe offer a prayer that God will send someone else to reach them. But if we truly love them, it will not be an effort for us to invest or share our lives with them. And see if this is not true in your own life. It would seem to me that the more I share my life with someone, the deeper my love grows for him or her.

Prayer thought: Father, soften my heart this day toward others. Lord, show me that person in need of Your love. Increase my love for him to the point that I begin to take interest in his life and circumstances. Let me be gentle in my dealings with him, showing him Your gentle and loving Spirit.

A Good Relationship with Him Makes for Better Relationships with Them

"Ask and it will be given to you; seek and you will find; knock and the door will be opened to you. For everyone who asks receives; he who seeks finds; and to him who knocks, the door will be opened. Which of you, if his son asks for bread, will give him a stone? Or if he asks for a fish, will give him a snake? If you, then, though you are evil, know how to give good gifts to your children, how much more will your Father in heaven give good gifts to those who ask him! So in everything, do to others what you would have them do to you, for this sums up the Law and the Prophets." (Matthew 7:7-12)

We are all relationship seeking. God deposited that need for relationship within us. God also seeks to have relationship with us. In our focal verses today, we see our God imploring us to seek a relationship with Him. "Just ask. Just look. Just knock. I'm here!" This is not a one-time thing that He's looking for. We are continually to ask, seek, and knock. We are to become dependent on Him to meet our needs and earnestly desire an ongoing relationship with Him, as a child with a parent.

He wants to bless us. Most parents want to bless their children. But neither God nor parents should be just the source we turn to when we want something. Parents can see through that in a heartbeat. So can God. But parents with strong, loving relationships with their children will bend over backwards to meet needs and desires in their children's lives. And since our capacity to love and to supply blessings is nowhere near our Heavenly Father's, how much more will He bless us! But remember, parents should learn to discern needs from selfish, harmful desires in their children's lives. We have to be able to determine when we should hold back some things from our children that we know are not good for them. Spoiled brats do not make productive adults. God does the same thing with us. Spoiled Christians do not make productive servants.

As we begin to develop a deeper, loving relationship with our Heavenly Father, we should begin to notice our relationships with others becoming sweeter. We know verse 12 of our passage today as "The Golden Rule." And it is a golden piece of advice. Actually, it is not advice. It is a command. And if we all lived by it every day, what a different world this would be. ***"Doing unto others as you would have them do unto you"*** requires sacrifice. It requires putting others ahead of yourself. It requires humility and obedience. But if we truly want to relate to others as Christ relates to us, it's a wonderful place to start.

Prayer thought: Lord, I realize today how important it is for me to continually seek and pursue a deep, personal, loving relationship with You. All the other relationships in my life are depending on it. I realize that being in that kind of a relationship with You not only means having my needs met and being blessed by my Heavenly Father, but it also means that You deposit in me the capacity to meet needs and to bless others. Thanks, Dad.

Overflowing Love

"Now may our God and Father Himself and our Lord Jesus clear the way for us to come to you. May the Lord make your love increase and overflow for each other and for everyone else, just as ours does for you. May He strengthen your hearts so that you will be blameless and holy in the presence of our God and Father when our Lord Jesus comes with all His holy ones." (1 Thessalonians 3:11-13)

Well, if we could memorize these verses and sincerely pray these words over the lives of our friends regularly, I believe we would begin to see some changes both in them and in ourselves. First of all, Paul was praying for the Lord to make it possible for him to return to the Thessalonian church. Do we pray for clear opportunity to reach specific people?
Sometimes it takes just a small opening for God to change someone's life for eternity. Ask God to give you that opening, and then let the Holy Spirit take over. Be careful, however, not to burst through that opening with a Bible on one hip and a Greek and Hebrew dictionary on the other trying to convince, explain, and force the gospel on your friends and family. I've prayed many times, as probably you have, for a certain person's heart to be softened so that he may receive God's gift of love, grace, and mercy. We need to be praying this prayer of overflowing love for *ourselves* and each other daily. *"May the Lord make your love increase and overflow for each other and for everyone else..."* What better thing could we pray for? As love increases; mercy increases, kindness increases, patience increases, understanding increases, tolerance increases...all of the things that love is as described in 1 Corinthians 13 and other places in scripture.

But the most important thing is that as love increases, Jesus Christ is lifted up before man. And John 12:32 records a promise made by Jesus Himself, *"But I, when I am lifted up from the earth, will draw all men to myself."*

Yes, we should pray for each other's specific physical, emotional, and spiritual needs. But we should also be praying this prayer for each other, that our love increases and that He strengthen our hearts to make "right" decisions. We can't make decisions for others, and they can't make decisions for us. All we can do is point each other in the right direction and pray that we turn the right way. As a friend, one of the most difficult things to watch is seeing someone whom we've been trying to help make a definite wrong decision that we know is going to bring trouble or heartache into his life. And when that heartache comes, to refrain from saying, "I told you so"—to just be there to point them in the right direction again and again and again if that's what it takes, to be non-judgmental and to continue to pray for them. That's overflowing love.

Prayer thought: Father, You've shown me today how important it is that we love each other and that we pray for increasing love. All of us need increasing love, increased to the point of overflowing. This week, Lord, let there be a visible difference in my love level. Open a door for me to pour that love through. And, Lord, I pray for great increase in love for (call out specific names) this week. Strengthen our hearts so that our decisions are birthed out of Your overflowing love.

Nobody Could Love Them...Could They?

"You have heard that it was said, 'Eye for eye, and tooth for tooth.' But I tell you, do not resist an evil person. If someone strikes you on the right cheek, turn to him the other also." (Matthew 5:38-39)

"You have heard that it was said, 'Love your neighbor and hate your enemy.' But I tell you: Love your enemies and pray for those who persecute you." (Matthew 5:43-44)

Have you ever had a difficult person to deal with? What constitutes a difficult person? Is it just someone who doesn't agree with you or refuses to cooperate with you? Maybe it's not really a difficult person at all, but rather a difficult situation involving an otherwise likable person. And after the situation is over, maybe your difficulties with that person will disappear. But sometimes...there are those people who are just major thorns in the flesh. People whom you can't seem to please no matter what you try to do or say. People who seem to delight in making your life miserable. People who seem to bring out the very worst in you. The dictionary's definition of "difficult" as it pertains to a person is "hard to please, satisfy, or manage." Are you getting a mental picture of anyone at this point? I would expect that most of us are.

Most of us have our own way of dealing with difficult people. Check out this list of reactions to see if you find your favorite: avoiding them (my personal favorite), confronting them, arguing with them, talking about them, or plotting against them. Maybe you could even add a few others. None of these reactions, however, are listed in our scripture verses for today. "Turn the other cheek?" "Love your enemies?" "Pray for those who persecute you?" That's very hard to do, Lord! I read somewhere that the best way to get rid of an enemy is to make him your friend. As Christians we shouldn't avoid the difficult situations or the difficult people who cross our paths, because it is in our dealing with them that God can teach us and work into us more of His character.

Loving the unlovely is a very "difficult" thing to do. Can we do it? Only through the power of the Holy Spirit. Our flesh will fight it every step of the way. When we are hurt, we want to hurt. When we are accused, we want to accuse. When we are yelled at, we want to yell back. Jesus knows that these are natural human reactions. But kingdom living includes reacting to difficult people and difficult situations in "super-natural" ways; such as turning the other cheek, going the extra mile, suffering in silence, praying for those who hurt us, forgiving and forgetting. And Jesus not only tells us how to do it…He showed us with His life. Remember Calvary?

Prayer thought: All right, Lord. I confess that my attitude and my actions toward (fill in a name) have not been what they should have been. I always saw <u>them</u> as the problem and didn' t recognize my response to them as a problem between You and me, Jesus. Thank You for Your example. When I am tempted, Lord, to react in the flesh, please bring these scriptures into my remembrance. Help me to love the unlovely, just as You love me!

Love Seeds

"Jesus called his disciples to him and said, 'I have compassion for these people; they have already been with me three days and have nothing to eat. I do not want to send them away hungry, or they may collapse.'" (Matthew 15:32)

The Bible speaks often about the principle of sowing and reaping. We know the importance of gospel seeds, sowing the Word, and sharing our faith. We're going to see today how important it is to sow "love" seeds. If we stop at just telling the story of Jesus, the cross, and the resurrection, we're not letting people know that there is an "everyday" Jesus for their lives. And in today's scripture we see Jesus as the compassionate, caring friend who recognizes needs, genuinely cares, and actively gets involved in lives. And that is the game plan for us. What an example for us to follow!

Love spoken is meaningful, but love demonstrated is powerful! The key ingredient to demonstrated love is genuine concern or compassion. Maybe our prayers in this area should not be, "Lord, show me what to do," but rather, "Lord, birth in me a true compassion for this person's needs." It is out of our true compassion that the true love of Jesus is shown to others. From there He will show you how to best minister to the person's physical, emotional, or spiritual need. I guess what I'm saying is that we should avoid empty or self-bolstering ministry "works." That is, doing something for somebody else to make you feel better about yourself, or to impress someone else, or as a duty requirement to God. And I would dare say that most people have been guilty of this from time to time. We know we *should* go by and check on that elderly aunt, but we don't really want to. So before we even get there, we already have an excuse prepared as to why we can't stay long. Or, it's our turn to drive the "Meals on Wheels" van, and we're thinking, "I'm glad I only have to do this once every three months." Or perhaps, a neighbor or someone in our church family has had an unpleasant experience, such as a death, divorce, loss of job, or an accident or illness. So, we make an obligatory phone call to let them know that we are aware of the situation and we tritely end the conversation with, "Call me if I can do anything," while inwardly we are hoping that they won' t. Have I hit a nerve yet?

People know when you really care about them, and those *sincere* acts of love and friendship are the ones that are going to make a difference in their lives. The fact that Jesus went to the cross is what made forgiveness possible for me, but the <u>reason</u> He chose to go is what drew me to Him…because He loves me and it shows.

Prayer thought: Lord, birth in me a true compassion for people. Make it a real, genuine, Christ-like compassion. I've seen today, Lord, that playing the game and going through the motions are not really enough. I want to plant genuine love seeds in the lives of people, seeds that will draw people to You and reap a genuine harvest.

See a Need, Meet a Need

"When Jesus landed and saw a large crowd, he had compassion on them, because they were like sheep without a shepherd. So he began teaching them many things. By this time it was late in the day, so his disciples came to him. 'This is a remote place,' they said, 'and it's already very late. Send the people away so they can go to the surrounding countryside and villages and buy themselves something to eat.' But he answered, 'You give them something to eat.'" (Mark 6:34-37)

In the verses preceding this passage we see Jesus and the disciples trying to get away by themselves for some rest. The time alone was short-lived. The crowd saw the boat and raced ahead of them to get to the place where they would be landing. Jesus was faced with the immediate needs of a lot of people. How did Jesus respond? Remember that He and His disciples were trying to find some solitude. He didn't look out and say, "Look at all those people. I guess I'd better do something to get rid of them." No, Mark says, *"he had compassion on them."* There's that word again. Compassion. Genuine concern. Genuine love. Genuine caring. He saw them as sheep needing a shepherd. He assessed their need at that time to be spiritual. He began to teach them. You may think, "Well, it's a lot easier to know what to do to help people when they are coming to you and asking for your help." Yes, it is and we certainly need to take advantage of those opportunities. But sometimes people are coming to us crying for help in less obvious ways because they don't want to be a bother. We need to live our lives in such a way that we don't give people the impression that we are too busy for them or that we don't really want to get involved in their problems. Just as Jesus did, we need to let them know that we are there and are willing to help.

After Jesus had been teaching for a long time, the disciples began to look around and assess the physical needs of the people. We need to do that also. It is hard to lead people into a deeper spiritual relationship when they have immediate physical problems or circumstances that need to be addressed. The disciples said, "Look, we've got five thousand people out here in the middle of nowhere. It's getting late and they're all hungry. We need to be breaking up this meeting so they can all go back to town and get something to eat." Jesus, recognizing another teaching opportunity here, both for the disciples and the crowd, very quickly told them to do something that was physically impossible. He said, ***"You give them something to eat."*** Now, I'm sure it would not have been quite so incredulous to them if He had said, "Don't worry, I'll take care of it." But He wanted the disciples to be "involved" in meeting this need that they had just recognized. There was another lesson here for the disciples. Because the task at hand was physically impossible on their own, they had to realize that if they were going to feed these people, supernatural help was going to have to come from somewhere. And that's the way it is with us today. God may show us a person to whom we should witness, or a need in a person's life that requires a lot of time and resources. We recognize that they have a need, but we don't think we have what it takes to meet it. So, we send them to the preacher, or the Sunday School teacher, or to some service organization designed to deal with that problem. Maybe that's one road to take, but it may not be the road God wants us to take. God just might want us to become actively involved. And if He does, He will make it possible. But we have to be willing.

Prayer thought: Father, I realize that the first step involved in meeting the needs of others is being willing. I also realize the next step is being able to see the need. Open my eyes, Lord, to the needs of the people You put in my path. After I recognize the need, open my ears that I might hear Your voice giving me the instruction I need to take the next step. And even if what You are telling me to do seems uncomfortable or even impossible, let me remember the story of Your disciples being actively involved in the feeding of the five thousand.

Leftovers Anyone?

"'How many loaves do you have?'" he asked? 'Go and see.' When they found out they said, 'Five—and two fish.' Then Jesus directed them to have all the people sit down in groups on the green grass. So they sat down in groups of hundreds and fifties. Taking the five loaves and the two fish and looking up to heaven, he gave thanks and broke the loaves. Then he gave them to his disciples to set before the people. He also divided the two fish among them all. They all ate and were satisfied, and the disciples picked up twelve basketfuls of broken pieces of bread and fish. The number of the men who had eaten was five thousand." (Mark 6:38-42)

Once you have prayed for compassion, been shown the need, and have yielded yourself to the Lord; pray for a plan. Obviously, distributing food to five thousand people required a plan. Jesus developed one. He told the disciples to gather up whatever food they could find. There's a lesson for us. We need to work with whatever we have. If you have an extra ten minutes to spend with someone on the phone who may need a friend, start with that. If you have an extra $10 to put gas in someone's tank, start with that. If you know a scripture passage that deals with a particular circumstance that someone is dealing with, start with that. Gather up your resources and give them to the Lord to multiply.

The disciples found five loaves and two fish. Details of the multiplication are not clearly given. It does say that Jesus directed the disciples on how to ready the people to best receive. People need to be in the right position and the right frame of mind to receive from God. If any of these people were out wandering around and not paying attention, they may have missed the basket when it was passed around. After Jesus had the people settled and the organization established, He took the food from the disciples. He looked toward heaven. There's a great piece of advice. Before we attempt to do anything for someone else, we need to look toward our source of strength and thank Him for it in advance. Jesus then took the food and gave it to the disciples to give to the people. Here again, He could have just had the food appear in the groups. He could have personally delivered it to each group. But He wanted the disciples actively involved in this act of compassion.

At the end of our passage today, we are told that after everyone had eaten and were satisfied, the disciples picked up twelve basketfuls of broken pieces of bread and fish. So, when you're asking God to give you compassion for someone and a plan to meet his need, why not ask God to multiply it. I'm sure someone can benefit from the leftovers!

Prayer thought: Lord, after You've shown me a need, I'm asking that You show me Your plan. Lead me in the practical steps I can take in the natural realm in order for You to show Yourself to others in a supernatural way. I thank You in advance, Jesus, for Your perfect plan and provision. Allow me to be actively involved in that plan. Thank you, O Lord, that You are not only a God of provision, but also a God of abundance!

Check Your Worship Meter

"Yet a time is coming and is now come when the true worshipers will worship the Father in spirit and truth, for they are the kind of worshipers the Father seeks. God is spirit, and his worshipers must worship in spirit and in truth." (John 4:23-24)

Why do people go to church? If you posed that question to a random sampling of church-goers, you might get a variety of responses. Some might say, "I feel better when I go to church," or "I enjoy being with my Christian friends," or "I want my family to be in church." Others might tell you, "I'm expected to be there," "It' s a habit," or "I feel guilty when I don' t go." The worker bees might say, "I have to be there to teach or sing or keep the nursery." Those are all acceptable reasons. God will let you start with those or perhaps include them in your reasons for coming to His house. But He also wants us to reach the point where we truly come to WORSHIP the Most High God, the Creator of the universe, who just happens to be our own personal Lord and Savior, the One who changed our lives forever!

I'll be honest with you, I went to church off and on for a big part of my life strictly for most of the reasons we listed earlier. I came for either what I could receive from the programs set up by the church or to work in the programs set up by the church. When I was a teenager and a young adult, there were many times when I would come to Sunday School to be with my peers, and not even bother to stay for the worship service. It wasn' t until I reached my thirties as a single parent that I began to truly hunger and thirst for more of God Himself in my life, and not just the programs of the church. And as He began to reveal more of Himself to me through the Word, it became more and more *necessary*, *vital*, even *urgent* for me to WORSHIP Him. Yes, I still come to church to serve in the programs of the church, and sometimes I may still do some of them because I'm expected to. But I've learned that there is much more of God' s anointing on me (which means I am doing things in His power instead of my own) when my motives are pure and I'm there because I love Him and have come to meet with Him and to truly WORSHIP (an active verb) Him.

Check your worship meter. Our focal verse today says that God is seeking true worshipers. And I would say from experience that true worshipers are those who are seeking God and have discovered that He is truly worthy of our worship. Has worshipping God become necessary, vital, and urgent for you?

Prayer thought: Jesus, You are worthy of my worship! There is none like You. I praise You, Lord, for bringing me out of the darkness and into the light. I thank You for Your church, but I ask You to help me to see it not as a place to go, a program to attend or to work on, or a weekly obligation to fulfill, but as a gathering place for true worshipers of the Most High God! Lord, I want to be one of the kind of worshipers whom You seek.

Listen to Me, Look at Me

"And when you pray, do not be like the hypocrites, for they love to pray standing in the synagogues and on the street corners to be seen by men. I tell you the truth, they have received their reward in full. But when you pray, go into your room, close the door and pray to your Father, who is unseen. Then your Father, who sees what is done in secret, will reward you. And when you pray, do not keep on babbling like pagans, for they think they will be heard because of their many words." (Matthew 6:5-7)

"When you fast, do not look somber as the hypocrites do, for they disfigure their faces to show men they are fasting. I tell you the truth, they have received their reward in full. But when you fast, put oil on your head and wash your face, so that it will not be obvious to men that you are fasting, but only to your Father, who is unseen; and your Father, who sees what is done in secret, will reward you." (Matthew 6:16-18)

Prayer is another area of our worshipping God. An important part of our prayer life should be praise and adoration, an acknowledgment of who God is and how much we love Him and need Him. In fact, the model prayer of our Lord (Matthew 6:9-13) begins in this manner. In our first focal passage today, Jesus was speaking about the practice of public prayer by the Pharisees, praying before men to impress men. For those of you who do occasionally pray in public, it is very easy to be conscious of the fact that people are listening to you and to try to make sure you say things correctly. I've even heard preachers get in mini-sermons during their prayers. Come to think of it, I've probably done that myself, especially when praying before my children or my youth group. One of the most poignant statements I've ever heard to punctuate our scripture today was the story of the high-ranking community official who was asked to open the town meeting with prayer. After softly speaking to the Lord, another official chastised him because his prayer was not loud enough to be heard. The first man simply stated, "I wasn' t talking to you." Another area Jesus addresses here is "babbling." I'm quite sure I've been guilty of that one, also. We all know that person who we hope doesn' t get called on to close a service. Anyway, it' s good to know that we don' t have to be eloquent, lengthy, or perfect in our prayer time. The same God who listens to Billy Graham' s prayers is just as attentive to my bungled-up ones. The Bible also says that, even when we can' t find the words, God understands our groanings. Get alone with God. Worship Him in prayer.

The second area of worship that we are addressing today is fasting. You will notice that these verses don' t say "if" you should happen to fast, it says "when" you fast. It would seem then that it is a given that you will be fasting. But in a lot of our churches today, fasting is not as common an area of worship taught as is giving and prayer. Fasting was a part of Jesus' life. He did not teach it as a hard rule to be followed in order to prove your righteousness. Jesus fasted during those times when hearing from the Father and being close to Him were more important than eating. Fasting, prayer, and being alone with God go together as another means by which we may worship. Just giving up food for a period of time is not necessarily a worshipful fast. Jesus' statements about the Pharisees in our verses today evidence that fact. Jesus talked here about the need for fasting to be a private thing between God and us. We shouldn' t make it obvious to the world about our self-imposed sacrifice, or the world' s attention is all we will receive. But, if our purpose for fasting is to receive direction or strength from God, His word says that what is done in secret will be rewarded.

Prayer thought: Lord, I want to worship You because You are worthy of my worship. Help me to be aware of the fact, Lord, that even when I'm asked to pray in public I'm still speaking to You and not to those around me. Help me to remember, Jesus, that it is not my purpose to draw attention to myself. Develop in me, Lord, that need to get alone with You and block everything and everyone else out in order to draw closer to You.

Praying His Way

"This, then, is how you should pray. 'Our Father in heaven, hallowed be your name, your kingdom come, your will be done on earth as it is in heaven. Give us today our daily bread. Forgive us our debts, as we also forgive our debtors. And lead us not into temptation, but deliver us from the evil one.'" (Matthew 6:9-13)

Prayer is more than words. Yes, prayer involves words, but our words should reflect true attitudes of our heart. Today's focal passage is Jesus instructing us how to pray. It is not a lesson in memorizing magic words that automatically open the doors of heaven for us. The prayer in Matthew 6 is a model prayer showing us <u>elements</u> needed in our prayer lives, not just words to memorize and mumble back to God. Because the Lord's Prayer, or the model prayer, is on most churches' highly recommended memorization list as is John 3:16 and the 23rd Psalm, it is very easy for us to rush through the words without thinking about what we are saying. Let's read through this prayer today and examine the elements that I believe Jesus wants us to learn to incorporate into our own prayers.

"Our Father in Heaven" - We see several things in these few words. First of all, we see the word "our," which says to me that we are to acknowledge and hold dear to us the relationship we have with God. The only reason we can pray to Him in the first place is because He has provided a way for us to have a personal relationship with Him through His Son. And through Him we become His children and He becomes our Father. "Father" acknowledges what kind of relationship we have, father to child: not friend to friend, brother to brother, casual acquaintance, or occasional visitor in our lives. "In Heaven" tells us that we are not on equal ground. Our Father is the Creator of all things in this world, as we know it, and the King of Heaven we have yet to experience. And that brings us to the second element of the prayer.

"Hallowed Be Your Name"—What do these words signify that the attitude of our heart should be as we approach God? Reverence.

Respect. Awe. Recognition of His holiness. The name of God is to be revered and held in the highest esteem. The Word of God is clear about God's holiness and our need to recognize it. *(Read Exodus 3:5-6, 13-16, Psalm 5:7, Rev. 4:8)* I believe that when we see Jesus we will join the living creatures in crying, "Holy, holy, holy." And Jesus said, *"If you have seen me, you have seen the Father."* So, I want to start now to revere the holy name of God. Even if we are not in the habit of taking the Lord's name in vain, when we throw the name of God around casually or inappropriately, we are not recognizing the holiness associated with the name.

"Your Kingdom Come" - This is an acknowledgment to God that we are anticipating the Second Coming, that time when Satan's power over this earth will be replaced with the <u>total</u> acceptance of God's rule over heaven and earth. As believers we should be anxious for that day. The written Word of God ends, pointing to that day. *"He (Jesus) who testifies to these things says, 'Yes, I am coming soon.' Amen, Come Lord Jesus." (Rev. 22:20)*

"Your Will Be Done"—Submission is an important attitude for us to acquire in our prayer lives. Jesus showed us this quality in the garden as He prayed, *"Not my will, but thy will be done."* Asking God for His will to be done means taking our will out of the picture. Most of us want to pray our will to God and ask Him to see to it that it gets done. And it is okay to ask things of God specifically and to expect Him to hear and answer our prayers. But the final cry of our heart should be, "But if this is not right for me, God, don't give it to me. Because more than I want this particular outcome to this prayer, I want Your will to be done in my life."

"On Earth as It Is in Heaven" - We mentioned earlier about the ushering in of God's kingdom on earth. But until that day comes, we have to live on this earth. And if God's will is to be done on earth as it is in heaven then He is going to use you and me to accomplish it. The attitude of my prayer here is "Use me, O God."

"Give Us Today"—And here we get into the portion of prayer with which we are most familiar—petition, or prayer requests. Even

though God knows the desires and needs of our heart, it blesses Him to have us come to Him to supply them. Give us "today" or "this day" is an important part of this prayer because it causes us to recognize that we need God <u>every day</u>. God doesn't give us tomorrow's grace today.

"Our Daily Bread"—God promises to supply all our needs, but sometimes our perception of needs and His are two different things. *(Luke 12:29-31)*

"Forgive us our Debts"—Confession should be an important part of prayer. And yes, we have all prayed, "Forgive us of our sins." And in this model prayer Jesus instructs us to do that. But I think as we pray this way, we should stop and listen to see if God is pointing out any particular sin that He wants exposed and removed from our lives. We may already be aware of it; in which case, we should call it by name as we pray. *(1 John 1:8-9)*

"As We Forgive our Debtors" - This is not a suggestion; this is a condition of our own forgiveness. And here again, this is not just a mouthing of the words, "I forgive so and so." It is an emptying of our heart of the wrongs that we are holding on to, the bitterness of the instance, the blame that we have attached to that other person. After all, that is exactly what we have just asked God to do for us.

"Lead Us Not Into Temptation"—Dependence. We need to recognize that our flesh is weak and temptation is great. *(Matthew 26:41)*

"But Deliver Us From the Evil One"—God provides the way out for us. It is our job to obey those principles that He has established as our provision. *(1 Cor. 10:12-13)* Yes, we are all sinners and no, we are not perfect; but don't accept sin in your life as a natural outlet for your imperfection. Satan would like for us to have that attitude. Maybe that's why Jesus said we should pray, "Deliver us from the evil one."

Prayer thought: Lord, Your word has much to say about prayer. And I'll admit that sometimes I have felt as if my prayers were empty and ineffective. Thank You for teaching me about prayer. Help me to concentrate more on the attitude of my heart when I speak with You and less concerned about the eloquence of my words. Help me never again to look at the model prayer just as a scripture passage to be memorized, but as an example to be followed.

The End Was Just the Beginning

"When He had received the drink, Jesus said, 'It is finished.' With that, He bowed His head and gave up His spirit." (John 19:30)

The week preceding the celebration of Easter in most churches is commonly referred to as "Passion Week." It is a time of focus on the events of that week in Jesus' life that led up to the cross and, ultimately, the empty tomb. Different churches commemorate these events in different ways.

I have a friend who described her church's observance of Good Friday, or the day of the crucifixion. She told me that they completely strip the sanctuary of color and drape the altar in black, leaving the solemnness of the cross and His death a vivid picture in the minds of the congregation until they return on Easter (Sunday) morning. As they enter the sanctuary, they immediately see the contrast as the darkness has been replaced with life, light, color and the joy of the resurrection. My daughter attended a Maunday Thursday service with one of her friends where the church reenacted the Last Supper. While my son was in college, he attended a Christian campus organization that regularly had a three-night series of services depicting the events of Passion Week to prepare their hearts for the celebration of the resurrection they would experience at their various churches on the following Sunday. As youth leader one year, I led a Wednesday evening service prior to Easter that turned out to be very moving. We met in a large room upstairs in our church. I talked about the fact that we were gathered in an "upper room" and how vividly Jesus made His presence known to His disciples, preparing Himself and them for His impending death. We were there seeking His presence that night. We sat in a circle on the floor and each youth had a red candle sitting in front of him. A white candle ringed with a circle of thorns was placed in the center of the youth circle. Each person had a passage of scripture to read from the gospels beginning with the prayer at Gethsemane and ending with Jesus' declaration on the cross, "It is finished." Before the service began, I instructed them that we would light the candles and turn out the overhead lights. From that point on, there would be no other words spoken in the room except the Word of God from the scriptures they were reading, and the appropriately chosen songs that were played before and after the readings. We began. As each youth finished his scripture, he blew out his candle. As my son finished the story of the cross by saying, "It is finished," the white candle was left burning in the center of the room. We sat silently as we played two more songs. As the last note died out, I blew out the flame of the white candle and we sat in darkness. I had told them earlier that they were free to leave at that point whenever they felt like it, but there were to be no words spoken until they descended the stairs. But after the candle was blown out, no one moved for a very long time. The Holy Spirit was present and speaking to our hearts.

The purpose of that service was for us to get in touch with the innocence of Jesus, the sacrifice He made, the suffering He endured, and our own sinfulness that made it necessary. But although the earth itself cried and shook and darkness enveloped the land on that day, the story didn' t stop there…He arose! It was the resurrection that completed the plan of salvation freely offered to you and me. Without the resurrection—the birth, the healings, the teachings—even the cross would have had no lasting meaning. They would have all been faded memories by now, just a part of history. It is the fact that Jesus not only lived, but also continues to live that touches and changes lives forever. It was His victory over death that allows me to be assured of mine!

Prayer thought: Living Lord Jesus, how thankful I am that because of Your sacrifice on the cross, my sins can be forgiven. How overjoyed I am that Your resurrection paved the way for mine! But more than that, what an awesome thought it is that each day I have the privilege of serving a living Savior!

Crystal Ball or Lord of All?

"For I know the plans I have for you, declares the Lord, plans to prosper you and not to harm you, plans to give you hope and a future." (Jeremiah 29:11)

How many of us would like to know what our future holds? What are we going to be doing five, ten, fifteen years from now? What little twists and turns and ups and downs are in store for us? Maybe there are some things we would like to know, but probably a lot of things we wouldn't. The practice of performing ultra-sound procedures on expectant mothers to discover the sex of the unborn child is now common. That wasn't the case when my children were born. You had to have names ready for both a boy and a girl, decorate the nursery in neutral colors, and just wait. Personally, I enjoyed the excitement of the delivery room announcement. And even now, with the ultra-sound determination so readily available, there are still some parents who prefer not to know in advance. Even so, there are some naturally progressive things in our lives that we should plan for. We know that if we live long enough that we will reach an age where it will not be possible for us to continue working at our present jobs or at our present pace. We should plan for our retirement years. Those with children know that they will not stay small forever. Some days that may make us sad, and some days it may make us glad. I look back at my life and remember what it was like to have three small children hanging around my ankles, and now they are all adults and my "baby girl" is six inches taller than I am! What we used to think of as our future has a way of rapidly becoming our present.

Sometimes, however, it is not such a good idea for us to look too far ahead because it can become overwhelming, especially if we are currently involved in a set of bleak circumstances. That's when we need to lean on God's promise above and His promise of sufficient grace to handle one day at a time. I do know that there were a lot of things in my life that I spent too much time worrying about that are over and even forgotten now. Looking back, I see now that I should have put more trust in God and allowed Him to supply more confidence in me that He would take care of those worrisome issues. There were some good decisions and some bad decisions made on my part that probably changed the course of my life and the roads I've taken to get where I am today. But the final destination of my life was based on a decision I made a very long time ago to accept Jesus Christ as my Savior and Lord. And it was because of that decision that I don' t have to worry about my eternal future or my ultimate destiny.

Have you made that decision about your future? Can you count yourself as one who is included in the promises that God has made to His children? Maybe there are some things in your future you would rather not know, but where you are going to spend eternity should not be one of them. When you allow God to secure your future by accepting Jesus Christ as your Lord and Savior, it is much easier to deal with the twists and turns of this earthly journey.

Prayer thought: Father, I thank You for the promises in Your Word that You are in charge of my future. Give me wisdom to plan for the things that I should plan for and the trust to allow You to take care of the things that I can' t foresee. Help me, Lord, to live my life before others (believers and non-believers) in a way that <u>demonstrates</u> the confidence I have placed in You to handle all of my present and future circumstances.

If I Only Knew About Tomorrow

"Concerning the coming of our Lord Jesus Christ and our being gathered to him, we ask you, brothers, not to become easily unsettled or alarmed by some prophecy, report or letter supposed to have come from us, saying that the day of the Lord has already come." (2 Thessalonians 2:1-2)

As we study Paul's letters to the Thessalonians we note that they contain several references to the return of Christ. We find in 1 Thessalonians that although we know it is coming, we cannot be certain when it will occur. We do know that each generation gets closer and closer. We see prophecies being fulfilled and events occurring that could be "signs of the times." That shouldn't frighten us (unless we are not saved); it should excite us.

Think about this hypothetical question for a moment. If you knew for a fact that Jesus would be returning tomorrow, what would you do today? Most of us would hurriedly contact family members or people whom we care about that we know are not saved. We might spend the day fasting and praying. We might go home and start throwing away things we have that we know are displeasing to God in a desperate attempt to clean up our act. Perhaps we would try to contact people with whom we have had broken or strained relationships to try to make things right. Maybe we would stand on a street corner and pass out tracts to as many people as possible. What would you do?

The point is that we really don't know that Jesus' return will be tomorrow. On the other hand, we really don't know that it won't be either. Each day is a new day from the Lord. Each day could be our last day on earth and our first day of eternity. We know that each day since our regeneration or "new birth" experience, that the Lord has been changing us and preparing us for that day when we will be totally transformed into His likeness. The changing process is slower with some of us primarily because of our resistance to it. Some have made procrastination a dear friend. We will give up this habit someday. We'll witness to that person some other time. We'll go to church next Sunday. We'll pray about that later. We'll start a regular devotion time when this crisis is over. Procrastination hinders the Lord's ability to change us from glory to glory as He prepares us and uses us to prepare others for His return. So you see, it's not our job to predict or to be fretful about the time of His return. It is our job to live our lives faithfully and consistently in ways that demonstrate our relationship with Him. Go back to your "list" of things you would do if you only knew about tomorrow and start doing them! Stop procrastinating!

Prayer thought: Yes, Lord, I see now that I have been living my life as if I have an unlimited number of tomorrows. Show me the areas in my life where I have been procrastinating. Show me specific people that I need to tell about You. Help me, Lord, not to hinder Your changing work in me by holding on to things that slow down that process. Remind me, Holy Spirit, that I am not to live a sedentary life waiting for the rapture of the church, but I am to stay busy with Your assignments until that day or the day You call me home.

Please Open The Door!

"Here I am! I stand at the door and knock. If anyone hears my voice and opens the door, I will come in and eat with him, and he with me. To him who overcomes, I will give the right to sit with me on my throne, just as I overcame and sat down with my Father on his throne." (Revelation 3:20-21)

There is an annual event in our community called the Mayor's Prayer Breakfast. Organized by a group of Christian businessmen, it has become a very well-attended social function. It has grown so large, as a matter of fact, that it is necessary to meet in the sports/concert arena of our city. Tables are set up in the arena, and groups of people from all walks of community life gather for breakfast and to hear a guest speaker. I attend most years with a group of people from my secular workplace. Churches also reserve tables and sit together for this event. A lot of us there are used to attending events with large gatherings of Christians where the gospel is preached and Jesus is exalted. However, this prayer breakfast has become a major social event where people come to see others and to be seen. It's attended by a lot of the area's business leaders, politicians, professors, professional people, as well as the area's churches. I am not sure that it is primarily a Christian group. I am quite sure that the hard-hitting gospel message presented by a handpicked "celebrity" may be one that some have never heard before, or at least do not hear on a regular basis.

In 1995, the guest speaker was a former astronaut. Yes, he talked about walking on the moon, but he was more passionate about sharing with us how Jesus Christ had changed his life and had restored his family. He presented a question to the crowd as he ended his "speech." "Do you have a personal relationship with Jesus Christ? Have you ever made the decision to ask Him to be the Lord and Savior of your life?" He did not give an altar call, but there were response cards on the table. Did anyone sign one? Did anyone privately make that decision that morning? I don't know. But I will say that everyone there who had never made that decision for Jesus did make a decision that day. Making no decision for Jesus is making one against Him. Each time someone is presented the opportunity to open the door of his heart to Jesus—whether by a preacher, teacher, friend, family member or even in the privacy of his own home by the reading of the Word, or some other material (maybe the words on this page)—when the time comes to decide, a non-decision is a decision of rejection. And even though God is a loving and merciful God, there are just so many times that He will ask. Every rejection is another hurt. It's like another blow with the hammer to the nails in His flesh. The reason it hurts so much is because Jesus knows the outcome of rejection—eternal separation from God.

Have you responded to the plea of Jesus stated in today's title? Have you opened the door? If not, this is yet another opportunity for you to make the life-changing decision to make Him Lord of your life. Remember, not saying "yes" is saying "no."

The prayer for today is a prayer that will open the door of your heart to the one knocking and will be the greatest decision that you've ever made. Even if you have a religious or church background, deep down you know whether or not you've really opened the door for Him. You know whether or not you have a <u>personal</u> relationship with Jesus or are just a social church-goer like those described at the prayer breakfast. If you are willing, He is ready. Speak the words of this prayer from your heart and you can say, "Today I made a decision for Jesus!"

Decision Prayer: "Jesus, today I hear You knocking on the door of my heart. I know that I am a sinner, but that You loved me enough to die for me. Today I am inviting You into my life to cleanse me, change me, and take control of my life. Lord Jesus, I am deciding today that this is the first day of the rest of my life as a Christian!

If you made a decision for Christ today, let me be the first to say "Congratulations"! Welcome to the family of God! If you have been a Christian for a while, I pray that this book has stirred a passion inside of you to continue "Soaring with Excellence"!

Deborah Cox

About the Author

With over a decade of experience in Christian teaching ministry, and a life-time of highly relatable life experiences, Deborah Cox has presented practical application of God' s Word to hundreds of individuals in numerous adult and youth group settings. Those who have sat under her tutelage have gleaned from her down-to-earth examples, and thought-provoking challenges in living the Christian life. Several of her students are now pastors, teachers, and missionaries.

Cox is a member of Cape First in Cape Girardeau, MO, where she continues to learn and grow, having graduated from their 30 week "School of Leaders" course. She currently leads two weekly cell groups, as well as assists with the writing and directing of their major drama productions.